They Sailed from Plymouth

JACYNTH HOPE-SIMPSON

They
Sailed from
Plymouth

HAMISH HAMILTON

LONDON

First Published in Great Britain
by Hamish Hamilton Children's Books Ltd 1970
90 Great Russell Street London W.C.1
© *1970 Jacynth Hope-Simpson*

SBN 241 01880 3

To Ian and Daphne

Printed in Great Britain
by Ebenezer Baylis and Son, Limited
The Trinity Press, Worcester, and London

Contents

Part One *The Golden Lands*

Part Two *The New World*

Part Three *An Unknown Land in the South*

List of Illustrations

Map of Captain Cook's Voyages.

Author's Note

I would like to thank for their help:
Mr W. Best Harris, Chief Librarian, Mrs M. Beckford, Local History Librarian, and Mr K. Burns, Naval History Librarian of the Plymouth City Libraries; Mrs Hazel Berryman of the Plymouth City Art Gallery; Dr Quentin Bone of the Marine Biological Association of the United Kingdom; Mr Eric Davies of the *Western Morning News*; Mr Colin Dixon, Organising Secretary of Mayflower 70; and Prebendary J. K. Cavell, Vicar of St Andrew's, Plymouth.

J.H–S.

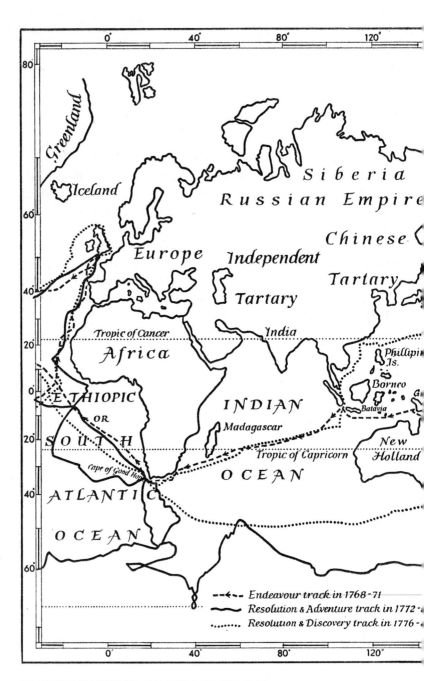

	0°	40°	80°	120°

Greenland

Iceland

Europe

S i b e r i a

R u s s i a n   E m p i r e

Chinese

Independent

Tartary

Tartary

Tropic of Cancer

Africa

India

Phillipi
Is.

E T H I O P I C

Borneo

OR

INDIAN

Batavia

S O U T H

Madagascar

New

Tropic of Capricorn

Holland

Cape of Good Hope

O C E A N

A T L A N T I C

O C E A N

0°

--◄-- Endeavour track in 1768-71
———— Resolution & Adventure track in 1772-
.... Resolution & Discovery track in 1776-

	0°	40°	80°	120°

MAP OF CAPTAIN COOK'S VOYAGES

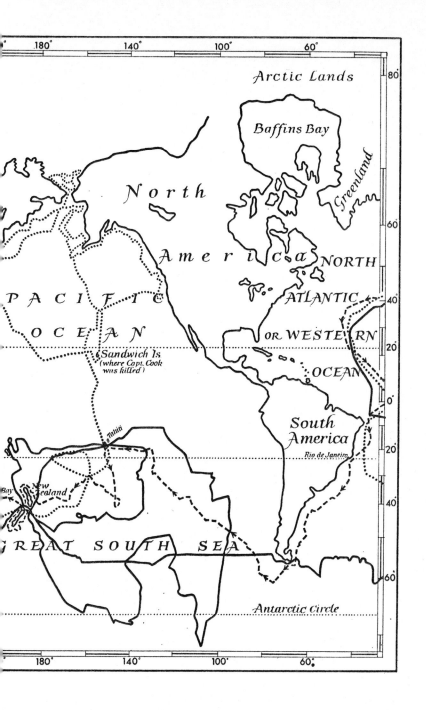

PART I

THE GOLDEN LANDS

"To seek new worlds for gold, for praise, for glory."
Sir Walter Ralegh,

The Ocean's Love to Cynthia.

I

An Arrival

IN THE year 1501, a fifteen-year-old Spanish girl set out to be married. She sailed up the Atlantic coast of France, into the widest part of the English Channel, and then came to Plymouth Sound in the far south-west of England. England was to be her new home, so she watched anxiously to see what it was like.

The prevailing south-westerly winds drove her ship past Penlee Point and into a magnificent bay. It was some five miles across at the mouth, and more than three in depth to the cliffs on the foreshore. On the western shore were hills covered with trees; on the eastern, the cliffs rose up into gorse-covered downland. Two rivers stretched deep inland from either side of the bay.

The girl knew that she was going to Plymouth, and so she stared around to see just where Plymouth was. The mouth of the larger river; the Tamar, the seamen called it; was marshy, so it could not be there. She could see an inlet, with what seemed to be mills worked by the tide fixed across it. She could see a little chapel up on the grey cliffs of the foreshore. Somebody told her that the foreshore was called the Hoe, and that the chapel was dedicated to her own patron saint, St Katherine. Then the Spanish girl saw the town.

They sailed close inshore as if they would go up the mouth of another river, the Plym. Instead, they went through a narrow gap to an inlet hidden behind the cliffs of the Hoe. The sailors on board knew that this was an ideal harbour, sheltered from the south-westerlies that blew in from the Atlantic. The town of Plymouth was huddled around the port. At the mouth of the harbour stood a castle with four towers, to protect the town from attack by sea. The girl's first impression was one of greyness. Most of the main buildings were made of a local limestone. It does not grow warm and mellow even in sunshine. When it is wet, it gleams, and looks hard as marble.

They anchored in the harbour, which was called Sutton Pool. It was busy with shipping, both fishing boats and small merchant ships. Plymouth was a moderately important place, though far surpassed by the ports of London and Bristol, as well as by other places in Devon, like Dartmouth. The ships were quite small, with probably none over eighty tons. This meant none could carry more than eighty large barrels of wine.

At that moment, the decks of the ships were crowded with sailors. The quaysides were thronged as well. They were all waiting for someone. The girl took a deep breath, and straightened her shoulders, because she knew they were waiting for her. One day, she would be Queen of England.

The girl was a princess, and her name was Catherine of Aragon. Her parents were King Ferdinand and Queen Isabella of Spain. She had come to marry Prince Arthur, the heir to the English throne.

As Catherine stepped ashore, she was greeted with ceremony. It was suggested she go to church to give thanks for her safe arrival. Long sea voyages were unpleasant things, and safety could never be taken for granted. They set off uphill to a church on the outskirts of the town, which was dedicated to the fisherman saint, St Andrew. The streets were narrow, with houses that were three or four storeys high. They pressed closely around her, the upper storeys overhanging the ground. The houses were built of grey stone, or of daub, whitened with limewash. The wooden doors and window frames were heavily ornamented and carved. The latticed windows, often covered with waxed paper, not glass, only let in a little light. Inside, the houses were made darker by more wood; massive beams, or carved panelling. As the horses' hooves clattered noisily over the cobbles, Catherine saw through an open door to a tiny walled garden behind one of the houses. There were glimpses of crooked roofs and chimneys, and of the sea below.

While Catherine glanced around, people were staring at her. They crowded at doorways and windows. One of the people who saw her may have been the young son of a Plymouth merchant. The boy's name was William Hawkins.

After the service at St Andrew's, Catherine was taken to Palace Court, the best house in the town. Once again, she had an impression of grey stone: the paving of the courtyard, more flagstones on the floors downstairs, the open fireplaces where huge logs were burnt. In her bedroom, the wide floor planks were laid straight on to the beams below. Flickers of light, the sound of talking, came up through the cracks.

Then Catherine left Plymouth, with its soft, damp air and its smell of sea water, tarred rope, and fish. She set off towards London. She travelled through deep, muddy Devonshire lanes, past orchards and cider presses, farmyards and water-mills. On the skyline was the rocky outcrop of Dartmoor, bleak and barren, and often hidden in mist. Sometimes she passed a manor house, set in a steep, lushly-wooded valley. The name of its owner would have meant nothing to her, for these West Country gentlemen were of mainly local importance. Names like Ralegh, Grenville, Gilbert, Champernowne, Gorges had not yet been heard at the court of Spain.

So the fifteen-year-old princess jogged on her way, weary, and probably apprehensive. She could not know that three separate threads in history were starting to come together. The first was that, nine years earlier, under the patronage of her own parents, Christopher Columbus had discovered America. The boundaries of the known world, for so long focused on Europe, had suddenly become wider. People were starting to look out across the Atlantic.

The second thread would be tragic for this young girl. She would marry, and shortly be widowed. She would then marry her brother-in-law, who would come to the throne as Henry VIII. In time, he would divorce her, and break with the Roman Catholic church in order to do so. It was the start of long years of tension between England and Spain.

The third thread was that, in Plymouth, there lived a family called Hawkins.

Very soon, these three threads would come together. They would make the small port of Plymouth famous all over the world.

2

Travellers' Tales

HENRY VIII, Catherine's husband, came to the English throne, and the small boy called William Hawkins grew up in Plymouth. It was soon obvious that he was an able and energetic person. By 1523, he was, as the tax returns show, the fourth richest man in Plymouth. He lived in a house in Kinterbury Street, between St Andrew's and Sutton Harbour. He had plenty of servants; pewter, or even silver plates for his meals; and a fine feather bed with heavy hangings to sleep on. He became Treasurer of Plymouth. Later, he was to be twice Mayor, and to sit in three Parliaments. He sounds like a typical, successful, small-town merchant. He was, and he was also something much more.

England, in Hawkins' time, was a small, rather backward country on the extreme edge of Europe. Compared to France and Italy, it was a fairly primitive place. Its chief business was farming, and its chief export was wool and cloth. English ships traded mainly with nearby places: the Low Countries and the French Channel ports. This meant sailors were used to short voyages in comparatively sheltered and shallow waters. They were never for long out of sight of land. There was no English tradition of long, deep-sea voyages, of launching out for weeks into deserted, uncharted seas. The exception was the Cabots, who had ventured across the Atlantic to Newfoundland. This had led to the finding of new fishing grounds, but to nothing else. Most English ships continued to hug the coasts. If English merchants wanted to send goods further afield, they hired ships from Germany or from Venice. Then William Hawkins began to wonder if this need always be so.

As a successful merchant, Hawkins had contacts abroad. He travelled to a number of ports in France, some of them still owned by England. He knew members of the English colony in the south of Spain. He met the captains of foreign ships which called in at Plymouth. And in such a little, tightly-packed town, he knew what the water-front gossip was. From all these, he heard talk of things that were still very little mentioned in England.

He heard stories about the Atlantic. For a long time, it had been a mysterious ocean, stretching westwards, as if for ever. Now it was known to have limits. For the first time since the days of the Norsemen, men were sailing across it. Columbus had crossed the Atlantic in search of a new route to the East. He had found a whole new continent of America, and had died still obstinately believing that he had reached the Far East. Then in 1520, Magellan had gone even further. He had sailed through a strait near the tip of South America, and out into the Pacific. He was killed on his homeward voyage, but one of his ships had sailed on, to go right round the world. Right round the world, while English ships just sailed up and down the Channel.

There was plenty of talk of America to be heard by a man who bothered to listen and ask questions. This vast continent was both a barrier on the way to the East, and something new and exciting in its own right. Some of the travellers talked about the beauty of the West Indies that had so excited Columbus himself. ". . . the sea full of islands to all the four winds, and all green and full of trees, the loveliest sight that eyes have seen . . . Always the land was the same beauty and the fields very green and full of an infinity of fruits, as red as scarlet, and everywhere there was the perfume of flowers, and the singing of birds, very sweet."

Hawkins was much more interested to hear what a trader could find in America. There was not only sugar and hides, but gold which lay in the beds of shallow streams or under the earth. The warm seas around the American tropics held pearls. Later, Hawkins' grandson, Richard, described one of these pearls. It "is called La Peregrina, being as big as the pommel of a poinard," that is, as the knob on the hilt of a dagger. That same pearl was recently sold in New York for over £15,000.

Mixed up with all this, there were stories of treasure. The Spaniards had conquered Mexico, then Peru. The ancient cities of the Aztecs and Incas held gold and silver and jewels. It was hard for Hawkins to tell where truth merged into fantasy.

As he listened, Hawkins wondered. What part could England play? If the Spaniards and Portuguese had their way, they would keep all these wonders to themselves. Pope Alexander VI had divided the New World between them by a decree. He said that anyone who infringed it would "incur the indignation of Almighty God, and his holy apostles, Peter and Paul". But, as Hawkins heard from his contacts, the French were already trying to stake out their own claims in America. When was England going to act? There was no lead coming from London. The famous men of the day were very slow to see the significance of the new discoveries, apart from a few, such as the great Sir Thomas More. The idea built up in Hawkins' mind that he himself might be the first to move.

Living in Plymouth, right in the far south-west, he had been badly placed for trade with France and the Low Countries. Ships from Plymouth had to sail all the way up-Channel, nearly the whole width of England. Worse, they had to sail back again against the south-westerly winds. The square-rigged ships of that time could not sail as close to the wind as a modern vessel, and they had so many ropes that every change of tack was a laborious business. Now, with the opening up of the Atlantic, Hawkins could see that Plymouth was in an ideal position. The west wind would be their ally. While ships from other English ports were still struggling down the Channel, Plymouth men could be out on the open seas. Early in the next century, John Smith was to say as a joke that it took as long to sail from London to Plymouth as from Plymouth to America.

So, in 1530, Hawkins equipped one of his own ships, the *Paul of Plymouth*. She was a big vessel for those days, of two hundred and fifty tons. We do not know much about the men who sailed with him, but like most sailors then, and for years to come, they were probably men who were not doing well on land. A bright boy who was making money did not go to sea as a common sailor. They may have been fishermen's sons from some narrow, stinking alley in Plymouth, or perhaps the sons of a farm labourer on Dartmoor, who despaired of wringing a living from that harsh and desolate land.

Hawkins set sail southwards, past the southernmost tip of Europe, and sailed on to Upper Guinea, now Liberia, in West Africa. The way was strange to himself and his crew, so at some point he took on a pilot. The pilot would have been French, or possibly Portuguese, for the English did not yet know these distant waters. Hawkins landed in Guinea. As they went in through the surf, the sailors were struck by the violent heat, and the cloying dampness. After a day or so on shore, they saw that the plants grew almost visibly. Compared to this, the air of Plymouth was gentle and kind.

Hawkins traded with the Negroes, buying ivory and probably pepper from them. As there were no means of preserving food, things were often eaten in a decaying or rancid state. Pepper and spices which helped to disguise the taste were all very highly prized.

From Guinea, Hawkins sailed across the Atlantic to Brazil. He established friendly terms with the natives, and traded with them. This time he was buying wood. It sounds a heavy and bulky cargo to carry in a small ship. The point was that Brazil wood, after which the country was named, yields a fine dye. This made it valuable in a country like England whose own export trade was centred round wool and cloth. Then Hawkins set sail for Plymouth again. To bring home one ship sounds a fairly modest achievement, but this venture of Hawkins was the start of English trade across the Atlantic.

We know about Hawkins' voyage because of the work of Richard Hakluyt, a remarkable and dedicated man. He did a great deal of propaganda to encourage exploration, and he also collected accounts of notable voyages that had taken place. Once he rode two hundred miles to talk to the last survivor of an expedition about his experiences. Sometimes he put the story together himself, but many of his accounts are first-hand ones and bring in the sort of detail which no one would mention unless they had actually been to a place. As one reads Hakluyt's collection it is possible to imagine some old seafarer talking, while the candles gutter low and the wind howls outside.

Hakluyt also describes Hawkins' second voyage. The trade in dyewood proved profitable, so he set off again in 1532. Once again he got on good terms with the natives of Brazil, and it was suggested that one of their kings should go back to England with him. We shall never know if this was Hawkins' own idea, or whether the king himself felt an urge to travel. A sailor called Martin Cockeram of Plymouth was left behind in Brazil as a hostage until the king should return.

When they reached England, Hawkins took the Brazilian king to Henry VIII at Whitehall Palace in London. Hawkins realized that one Plymouth merchant alone could not start regular trans-Atlantic trade. He must interest people with more wealth and influence than himself. Maybe the sight of a real, live Brazilian king would stimulate them.

The Brazilian king had no influence on English policy, but the sight of him caused nearly as much excitement as would a visitor from outer space nowadays. Hakluyt described him. "In his cheeks were holes made according to their savage manner, and therein small bones were planted, standing out an inch from the said holes, which in his own country was reputed for a great bravery. He also had a hole in his nether (lower) lip, wherein was set a precious stone about the bigness of a pea. All his apparel, behaviour and gestures were very strange to the beholders."

The king stayed in England for nearly a year, and Hakluyt says that he saw all he wanted to. He was obviously an enterprising and a brave man. Then they set sail for Brazil again, and unfortunately the king died at sea. As the ship approached the coast, the English wondered how they could break the news. What would happen to Martin Cockeram whom they had left as a hostage? When they landed without the king, Cockeram himself shivered. He need not have worried. The Brazilians recognized Hawkins' good faith, and knew that he had meant no harm to the king. They let Cockeram go back to Plymouth with the rest of the crew. He was still living there a few years before Hakluyt wrote his account of the voyages. It is a pity that Hakluyt was never able to talk to him. What did he do during that year in Brazil? He may well have been the first Englishman to stay a year on the American continent. And what of this first native American ever to come to England? Did anyone ask what he thought of the clothes, behaviour and gestures of Henry VIII?

Hawkins may have made other voyages, but no records survive after 1540. All that we know of the rest of his life is that he was a prominent figure in Plymouth. He was much concerned in civic affairs, and represented Plymouth in Parliament. He died about 1554.

Hawkins is usually known as "Old" William Hawkins, to distinguish him from his descendants. The name is misleading. It suggests a man past the height of his powers, or somebody set in his narrow, provincial ways. Hawkins should be remembered as a young and vigorous man, who seized an opportunity that few other people saw. Yet the name "Old" William reminds us of Hawkins' other great claim to be remembered. He founded a dynasty.

3

Hawkins of Plymouth

OLD William Hawkins' elder son was William
Hawkins the second. His son was William the
third. Old William's second son became Sir John
Hawkins, and his son became Sir Richard. They were
all descendants of whom Old William could have been
proud, but when we talk simply about "Hawkins of
Plymouth" we mean John.

John Hawkins grew up in a comfortable merchants'
house in Plymouth. He received a sound education, and
was used to seeing his family treated with respect in the
town. He heard talk of important business affairs. At his
father's table, he met sea captains with stories of strange,
foreign ports. He heard what was happening up in
London, in Parliament. When he grew up, he would be
able to take a part in public affairs, and to talk intelli-
gently to people whose concerns were in bigger places
than Plymouth.

Old William was a richer man than some of the West
Country landowners who struggled to hang on to their
estates. He had no intention of getting fancy ideas. Let
gentlemen's sons fritter money away at Oxford and
waste their time writing poetry. William, his elder boy,
was learning the family business, which he would take
over in due course. William could stay at the Plymouth
end, and in time, no doubt, would be Mayor and M.P.,
just as his father had been. Young John might as well

have a look at the places where the family fortunes came from. So, in a lucky moment for England, John Hawkins went to sea.

Sailing a ship was not considered a gentleman's occupation. It was hard and unpleasant work, and the crews were the most villainous gang you would find outside a prison. So when gentlemen went to sea in charge of a ship, they had a skilled navigator, or "master", to take care of all the work for them. Young John Hawkins, the merchant's son, was not protected in that way. He was at an age when people learn very fast. So he grew up to be a practical seaman. Years later, he had control of all the fighting ships of the nation. The politicians on one hand, and the ship builders on the other, tried to argue with him about costs and specifications. They were both rather disconcerted to find that Hawkins was not to be bluffed. He knew all about ships, and how they behaved, because he had learnt the hard way.

Old William died when John Hawkins was about twenty. A few years later, Elizabeth came to the throne. Hawkins was now ready to start his independent career. It was to take him far from his brother William, but the two brothers kept close links for the whole of their lives. This shows in both their financial dealings, and in a strong tie of friendship between them.

Like his father before him, Hawkins listened to talk of what was going on. Trade had developed fast since Old William's day. The West Coast of Africa was a free-for-all for traders. American trade, too, was growing. It was centred around the Caribbean, the sea between the West Indies and the coasts of Central and South America. A long stretch of this coast was known as the Spanish Main, that is to say, mainland. If the Spaniards could have their way, the whole Caribbean would be turned into a Spanish lake. The French, Hawkins heard, were challenging them, and harassing Spanish shipping.

When the Spaniards sent home a treasure fleet with the riches of Mexico and Peru, they had to travel in convoy with an escort of armed ships. The French were trying to strike into rich new markets, but why, Hawkins wondered like his father before him, why, why not the English?

Even when he was young, Hawkins was never a man to rush blindly into schemes without knowing what he was doing. If he wanted to bring goods back from the Caribbean, he would need to take something out there. The traditional English woollen cloth did not seem an ideal basis for trade in the tropics. From all he heard, what was needed out there was manpower. The Spaniards had taken out cattle and horses and hoped to turn the fertile West Indies into a vast ranch. They needed men for the sugar crop. Yet the whisper was that they were short of labour. The Spaniards themselves had killed some natives, and others had died of new, European diseases. The natives themselves made things worse. The Caribbean was named after a local tribe whom the Spaniards called the Caribs. And Carib, in Spanish, so Hawkins was told, simply meant cannibal.

Hawkins put all his intelligence sources together. The West Indies needed labour, and he knew a good source of labour. The West Coast of Africa was full of young, vigorous Negroes, whose physique put many a European to shame. He could take West Africans across to the Caribbean, and sell their services to the Spanish colonists there. Then he could buy sugar. This was greatly prized because, beet sugar not being known, honey was the only home-grown sweetener. He could buy ginger for flavouring food. He could buy hides from the cattle, and possibly pearls as well. Everyone would be satisfied.

There is no evidence whatsoever that Hawkins lost a single hour's sleep in wondering what the Negroes would think about it. Why should he have in that age? Hawkins was a good Protestant Englishman. He cared a great deal about the welfare of other good Protestant English-men, and treated his crews far better than was usual at the time. But he would have taken for granted that a Spanish Catholic was a creature akin to the devil. A Spanish Catholic would have assumed that Hawkins was eternally damned. If two white, European Christians could not see what a great deal they had in common, how could either of them sympathize with a black, African pagan? Both of them assumed that an African could have no soul at all, and therefore was nearer an animal than a human. It was reasonable to treat him as merchandise. To modern eyes, this may not excuse Hawkins. There is, however, a great deal of difference between not realizing something is wrong and between knowing quite well it is wrong and yet doing it all the same.

So, in 1562, Hawkins set sail from Plymouth. Like his father, he sailed down the hot, steamy African coast. He went to Sierra Leone where, says Hakluyt, "He got into his possession, partly by the sword and partly by other means, to the number of three hundred Negroes at least, besides other merchandise which country yieldeth." Then the winds bore him across to Hispaniola, the island that is now Haiti and the Dominican republic. Those same winds had helped Columbus to discover America, and indeed most of the early patterns of explora-tion and trade can be traced in the patterns of winds and of ocean currents.

In Hispaniola, Hawkins put the Negroes up for sale. He was right in thinking that they would be wanted. He was able to buy so much merchandise with the proceeds that he had to charter two more ships to carry it home. He returned to England "with much prosperous success and great gain to himself".

Having been so successful, commercially speaking, Hawkins planned a second expedition. He set out from Plymouth in 1564. Now that he had established himself, the Queen was prepared to help him. Her favourite method of sponsoring semi-official voyages was to give some practical help, but no money. If the voyage proved a success she would claim a share of the profits. The money she got in this way was spent on the needs of the Navy. In Hawkins' case what happened was that in addition to three ships of his own, he was lent a naval vessel, the *Jesus of Lubeck*.

Jesus? the sailors must have asked, and then been moved to some hideous blasphemies. For *Jesus* in spite of her name was a horrible ship. In a misguided fit of economy, Henry VIII had bought her second-hand from some German merchants in Lubeck. That was twenty-odd years ago, and she had been neglected since. In the first place she was, quite literally, rotten. She may have been built of unseasoned timbers, a not infrequent failing. Like all wooden ships, she was prey to worm. On top of that, her design made her very hard to handle. She was the classic type of old-fashioned, imposing ship, with very high structures fore and aft to make her look like a castle. The reason for this was that sea battles were still fought by ships getting very close to each other. Soldiers, who were carried on board, would then clamber on to the enemy ships for hand-to-hand fighting. These castle ships were obviously top-heavy, so they had to be made very wide compared to their length to stop them from toppling over. It was the exact opposite of stream-lining, and might carefully have been planned to offer the maximum wind resistance in an Atlantic gale.

Hawkins planned his voyage with great care. This was typical of him. He knew, like all master mariners, that a great many sailors died on long voyages of disease and lack of proper food. The usual answer was to take extra men, to replace the ones who died. Hawkins preferred to take fewer men, so that everybody had more to eat and better living conditions. This paid off, for his loss of men on this voyage was exceptionally low for this time.

Hawkins' balanced and sensible character is summed up in his sailing orders. "Serve God daily, love one another, preserve your victuals, beware of fire, and keep good company." "Serve God daily", meant attend daily prayers. Fashionable people might not be very religious, but the great seafarers, Hawkins, Drake and Gilbert, who lived very close to the elements and to death, were all genuinely devout. "Love one another" simply meant do not quarrel. When men were cooped up very close in a tiny ship, seeing no one but one another day after day, tempers could quickly flare up about little or nothing. As for "keep good company", it was probably advice to keep close together. This was very important at a time when there was not merely no radio, but no system of signalling by flags. Ships were usually unlit at night, and it was all too easy to drift apart.

The pattern of Hawkins' second voyage repeated that of his first. He sailed down the West African coast to Sierra Leone, where he took aboard several hundred Negroes. He then shipped them across to the Spanish Main. The local governors had received orders from Spain forbidding them to trade with English merchants at all. But Spain was a long way away, and they needed the men. This Hawkins seemed an obliging and reliable fellow to deal with. He was even taking orders for slaves and other goods to be delivered on his next voyage. So the governors paid, and everybody was happy. It would be another two hundred years before people asked awkward questions about how the Negroes felt.

The story of this voyage was told to Hakluyt by John Sparke of Plymouth. Sparke had observed the customs of some of the tribes he had seen. They were all vaguely referred to as "Indians" because Columbus had thought he had found the Far East. One tribe ate a strange vegetable, "the most delicate root that may be eaten, and do

far exceed our parsnips or carrots." Another tribe, up in
Florida, smoked "a kind of herb dried". It was not many
years before these habits spread to England. The vegetable was brought home by sailors, probably in one of
Drake's ships. Sir Walter Ralegh helped introduce it to
Ireland. He also helped to popularize the habit of smoking dried herbs. Ever since then, the British have eaten
potatoes and smoked tobacco.

Sparke had seen the tobacco being smoked on their
homeward journey. They had sailed up north to Florida
to visit a small French colony there. The colonists had
already had one English visitor, Thomas Stukely, who
had sailed out of Plymouth to join them. They had soon
come to wish that he had stayed home in England. When
Hawkins arrived, he was able to let them have some of
his own supplies of food. He offered to take them home
to France, but the colonists were determined to stay. This
was unfortunate for them. Soon afterwards, they were
massacred by the Spaniards.

For the Spaniards had decided to act. If they let matters drift on, the English and French would both get a
foothold in the Caribbean. It may well be that Hawkins'
second voyage, and his dealings with the Spanish ambassador later, were a planned attempt to get the Spanish
authorities to recognize English trade. If so, the attempt
was a failure. Hawkins was not put off. He would not
abandon a rich, new market so soon after he had found
it. He would trade lawfully if he could; but, if not, he
would go on trading. Who were the Spaniards that they
should have it all their own way?

Both sides were becoming bitter. The seeds of the conflict had been sown when Catherine of Aragon had
stepped ashore at Plymouth. In order to divorce her,
Henry VIII had separated the English church from the
Church of Rome. Ever since then, the religious difference
had sharpened all disagreements between England and

Spain. England was now ruled by a Protestant Queen, Henry's daughter. She was essentially a woman of this world, and very few rulers have understood this world better. The King of Spain was a Catholic, not merely in name, but in every part of his being. His vision was focused inwards, and up to the heavens. Trouble was smouldering between England and Spain. At each stage, the seamen from Plymouth would play their full part.

4

Treachery

RELATIONS with Spain were uneasy when Hawkins next sailed from Plymouth in the autumn of 1567. He had four merchant ships belonging to himself and his brother William. William, who was some twelve years older than John, was now settled in firm control of the Plymouth end of the family business. John also had two ships lent by the Queen; the *Minion* and, he was sorry to say, the *Jesus of Lubeck* again. The Hawkins brothers shook their heads doubtfully. They had had to spend a quarter of *Jesus*'s value to make her sea-worthy after her previous voyage. Would it prove to have been worthwhile?

Four days out of Plymouth, Hawkins knew that he would find out. The squadron ran into a fierce gale. The waves opened out into deep, yawning troughs, and *Jesus* pitched forwards violently as if she would dive right down into the depths. Then, with a shudder that made every plank in her shake and quiver, she was flung upwards again. Again and again, she plunged down and was flung up high. With all the heavy weight of her built-up decks the sailors could do no more than to keep her from toppling over. There was a violent creaking and tearing of planks as she started to wrench apart under the strain. Hawkins commanded the sailors to tear up the cargo of cloth they were carrying, and to stuff cloth into the leaks. He took a lantern and searched the ship, pray-

1. Palace Court, where Catherine of Aragon stayed,
demolished 1880

City Museum and Art Gallery, Plymouth; photo Tom Mollan

ÆTATIS SVÆ LViii
Ano Dni 1591

2. Sir John Hawkins, by Zuccaro

City Museum and Art Gallery, Plymouth

ing aloud as he did so. One gap looked worse than the others. The sailors told him that they had stuffed in no fewer than fifteen pieces of thick baize cloth.

Then the winds died down, and the sea became calmer. They were saved for the moment. Hawkins inspected the *Jesus* dubiously, and with none of that sense of affection that could grow up between a man and his ship. A ship with a high superstructure might be all right in an inland sea like the Baltic or Mediterranean. She was no use, Hawkins decided, for a long ocean voyage, and long ocean voyages were the thing of the future.

They sailed on to West Africa in search of another cargo of slaves. Hawkins had found that most native villages were by the banks of rivers. So at each river he came to, he would anchor his ships and then take to the small ship's boats. As they rowed upstream, the sailors talked about the strange things they saw. Were those really oysters growing on trees? Impossible, somebody else declared, and the argument raged. Then another man pointed out that the trees were standing in swampy ground. Once there had been water all round them, but now it had ebbed away, leaving the oysters behind.

Suddenly, there was a wallowing noise in the water, a loud thump, then splashes and shrieks of dismay. One of the boats had been overturned. As they stretched out oars to rescue their companions, the men in the other boats saw a huge, black creature swimming away. "It was a sea-horse," that is a hippopotamus, said Job Hortop. Job was the ship's gunner and had a particular interest in exotic plants and animals. Later, when he told his story to Hakluyt, he was full of comments about the strange and cunning habits of crocodiles, tigers, and snakes. There is something very infectious about Job's enthusiasm, even when one of the snakes had acquired two heads.

Hawkins was not so pleased about the way things were going. By the time he reached Sierra Leone, he had only a hundred and fifty Negroes. That was not enough to be worth undertaking the long voyage across the Atlantic. One of the Negroes, at least, had come willingly. He had been very friendly with his chief's wife, and thought it as well to leave before the chief found out. Then the king of Sierra Leone and another chief approached Hawkins. The Africans had been as quick as the Europeans to see that there was money to be made in the slave trade. This time, they had a suggestion to make. If Hawkins would help them to capture a neighbouring town, he could keep any prisoners. He did this, using his guns to set fire to the roofs of the thatched huts. Then, with another two hundred and fifty captives, he set sail for the Caribbean. It was not as many as he had been led to expect. There were dark murmurs among some of the crew that their temporary allies had eaten the rest of the captives.

Hawkins landed once more on the Spanish Main. At the first port, he found the authorities willing to trade with him. They reckoned that they knew what was needed out in America. Why should they take notice of some civil servant back in Madrid? At the next port, the authorities were not so obliging. They meant to obey the Spanish government, and refused to have any dealings with Hawkins. While he was wondering what to do, he was told that a Negro was very anxious to see him. The man was a slave, who had run away from the Spaniards. He could show Hawkins where the town's treasure was hidden. After this, everything went smoothly. Hawkins removed the treasure and then told the Spanish governor that he would consider it as the price of some Negro slaves he was leaving behind. He sailed away, leaving the governor to send in a report to Spain about what had happened. After a good deal of thought, the governor wrote that the pirate Hawkins had held the whole town to ransom. The treasure had been the price of everyone's safety.

Word was getting around. The governor of the next port was ready to help Hawkins to make a plan. Hawkins had got to land with a terrible show of brute force. He would wear full armour, to strike dread into everyone's hearts. His men would bombard the town. After that, they would have to trade with him in case even worse should happen. The governor and Hawkins went off to find a house to bombard. There was an old one, the governor said, where nobody was now living.

The last port Hawkins tried was fully fortified. He left it alone. He had done very well, and did not want to chance his luck further. The sensible thing was to get away from the Caribbean before the hurricane season came.

Then a violent storm struck them. Hawkins called it a "furicano". For four days, the *Jesus* was tossed and severely battered. He knew they would never manage to nurse her back across the Atlantic unless they could put in to repair her. They limped towards the Florida coast. The shallow channels were useless for shelter, and there was no fresh water. A Spaniard recommended them to a port in Spanish-owned Mexico. It was called San Juan de Ulua, St John of Ulua. Hawkins thought and decided that it was that, or nothing.

They sailed into San Juan. People came to the waterfront, and gathered on the decks of the other ships in the harbour. They seemed to be welcoming him. Suddenly Hawkins realized what had happened. The English flags were torn by the gales and all their bright colours were crusted with salt. No one could see what they were. The people in San Juan thought that his ships were part of the treasure fleet which came every year to take treasure to Spain. Hawkins looked quickly around. There was a long bank of shingle, like a small island, that commanded the harbour entrance. He ordered his men to take it before the Spaniards realized their mistake. At the worst, it would be useful to cover their retreat.

Hawkins tried to find a safe way out of the situation. He immediately sent envoys to Mexico City, two hundred miles away, to ask permission to stay to repair his ships and take on new supplies of food. With any luck he could be finished well before the treasure fleet came. That should not be for another month.

The treasure fleet came next morning. The English lookouts could see them far out to sea; huge, soaring vessels that looked like white towers on the waves. By the time they arrived at the harbour mouth, Hawkins would have to make up his mind what to do.

He knew very well that they would not look kindly upon him. He was an Englishman, "trading" by brute force. But England and Spain were not at war officially. The Queen might be happy to let her seamen harry the Spaniards, but she had no wish at all for an open conflict. If he let the fleet into the harbour, they might try to destroy him. If he kept them out, the incident could even spark off a war. Hawkins hailed the fleet, and suggested a compromise. He would let them come in if they would guarantee not to attack him. Each side could give the other twelve gentleman hostages.

The Spaniards agreed, and entered harbour. For a little while, all was well. Then the English sailors began to look uneasily at each other. Need all the ships in the harbour be quite so closely crowded together? Surely this was the traditional position for a sea-battle, which was fought by sailors boarding the enemy vessel and struggling hand-to-hand. The Spaniards had guaranteed safety, said somebody doubtfully. Why then were they so busy shifting their weapons and their big guns? How about that very large ship that was moored beside the *Minion* and the *Jesus*? Not many men appeared on her deck. Were there others, hidden inside?

Suddenly, a trumpet was sounded. Spanish sailors and soldiers appeared from all sides, trying to grapple their

way on to the English ships. The English defending the
island were taken by surprise. The Spaniards overwhelmed them, and captured the guns that were placed
there. They began to bombard the English, who fired
back in their turn. But Hawkins could see that, without
the island, which guarded the harbour approaches, he
had no chance of winning the fight. Could they with-
draw in safety?

Soon most of his fleet was captured, or damaged
beyond repair. He gave orders to the *Minion* and the
Jesus to draw free while they were still fighting. His
other remaining ship, the small *Judith*, was already edg-
ing her way out of the harbour. As the battle went on,
Hawkins manœuvred to place the *Jesus* as a shield to
protect the *Minion*. *Jesus*, shattered still worse by gunfire,
would never be sea-worthy again. For the time being, he
must try to keep her afloat. She contained most of the
valuables he had. What was more important, she had
food and water aboard. Already some of his sailors were
trying to transfer her cargo to the *Minion*. If they could
fight on for a little longer, he might manage to do the
rest under cover of darkness.

Hawkins was on board the *Jesus*. Suddenly, he heard a
cry of dismay. The Spaniards had sent in a fireship. This
was a common fighting device. An old ship was set on
fire and sent drifting towards the enemy's fleet. He knew
that if his own ships caught fire he would have no hope
of escape at all. The men on board the *Minion* had seen
the fireship as well, and had started to panic. They were
trying to draw her clear without bothering to wait for the
men on the *Jesus*. The fireship was coming nearer, and
Jesus was far too clumsy and bulky for him to move her
in time. The men still aboard her had launched the
ship's boats, and were rowing desperately to catch up with
the *Minion*. Hawkins gave a loud shout of command as he
realized that he himself could be left behind in the flurry.

He was one of the last to scramble on board. They dodged through the Spanish ships and sailed out of the harbour to where the other survivor, the *Judith*, was waiting for them. By dawn, without any warning or explanation, *Judith* had disappeared.

The *Minion* was crammed tightly with men, but there was not even food for a normal crew. For fourteen nightmarish days, they "wandered in an unknown sea", and lived on ship's parrots, and cats, and rats. When these were all eaten, they made soup by stewing up ox-hides. At last, in despair, they sought the land, not caring much who they found there. The place where they landed had no Spanish settlement, but no good food supplies either. With a resolution born of despair, Hawkins decided that they must get back across the Atlantic. Autumn had come again, and he dare not wait for the worst of the winter gales.

Some of the men could not face the prospect, and begged to be put ashore. They split into two groups, some walking north and some south. Both had a wretched fate. Of those who went north, only three got back to England. They claimed to have walked all the way from Mexico to Cape Breton in Nova Scotia, and were the first Englishmen to travel the North American coast. All the rest died, or were killed by Indians. The men who went south prospered at first, then the Spanish Inquisition began work in Mexico. They were condemned as heretics. Some were executed, and others, like Job Hortop, condemned to row in the galleys. After many years' slavery he escaped, and came home with tales of galleys and prisons in Mexico and in Spain. Being Job, he had other stories about earthquakes; dressing in grass to keep the sun off his body; eating exotic fruits like avocado pears; as well as some outsize snakes. He is the first of the ordinary Devonshire seamen that we hear speaking for himself.

Meanwhile, the wretched, starving *Minion* made her

way back across the Atlantic. Many men died. The first port they reached was Vigo in Spain, and Hawkins decided to risk putting in there. He had money on board, for he had taken gold off the *Jesus* before leaving San Juan. He managed to persuade the Spaniards to sell him food. His men snatched ravenously at fresh meat, and, in their weakened condition, some died of the sudden excess.

After three more hideous weeks, Hawkins knew that his crew would never be fit to sail the *Minion* home. He took twelve men on as crew from another English ship. With their help he struggled home to the nearest point of the English mainland, Mount's Bay near Penzance. Then, exhausted, he gave up responsibility for the moment, and sent a messenger off to Plymouth. The one thing that mattered was that he was alive, he and some fifteen other men out of the hundred-odd who had left San Juan. William could look after things now. William did.

When John Hawkins recovered, he began to take stock. All this need never have happened if it had not been for the *Jesus* needing repairs. The Navy ought to look after their ships better. They ought to design them better, for modern conditions. A narrower ship would manœuvre more easily, one lower in the water would not wrench herself apart. The events of San Juan de Ulua played a vital part in the ideas of England's future Treasurer of the Navy.

The episode had one other effect. The little ship called the *Judith* came home safely as well. Nobody knows to this day why she deserted Hawkins, or what she did on her long voyage home. Hawkins made one bitter reference to what happened when he said she "foresook us in our great misery". Otherwise, he remained silent, and probably only William knew what he really felt.

The captain of the *Judith* was a very impulsive young

man, who always liked to follow his own wishes. After San Juan de Ulua he hated the Spaniards with all the intensity of his passionate nature. At the time, this seemed unimportant, for he was only an unknown Devonshire seaman. Unfortunately for Spain, he was Francis Drake.

5

Revenge

DRAKE was a man born at the perfect moment. He came to his prime just as the English nation was beginning to feel its full strength, and was needing figures to be symbolic of its new vigour. One of these was the Queen herself, and Drake was to be another. He would be adored, hated, admired reluctantly all over Europe and in the new lands in America. Nobody was ever indifferent to him.

His beginnings looked unpromising, but they proved a part of his strength. He was born at Tavistock, some miles inland from Plymouth, on the fringes of Dartmoor. His father was a tenant farmer on the Earl of Bedford's estates. The elder Drake was a passionately convinced Protestant in the days before it was fashionable to be so. He was driven from his home because his neighbours were so hostile to him, and went to Kent. One strand in his son's character was already emerging. Drake, too, was fervently Protestant, which helped to sharpen his hatred for Catholic Spain.

Drake grew up beside the Medway, where his father became a lay preacher among the sailors at Chatham. Another important element in his future appeared. The son of the former inland farmer could now spend his boyhood messing about in small boats. When he was older, he went to sea in small coastal craft, engaged in local trade. His upbringing as a sailor was quite different from that of young men who sailed straight out into the open waters of Plymouth Sound. He learnt his craft in tidal waters, where sometimes you almost needed to smell your way through narrow channels with sandbanks on either side. He became one of the finest navigators of his age.

Drake was in his early twenties when he went back to Devon. He headed for Plymouth which, under the driving influence of the two Hawkins brothers, was fast becoming a major centre for ocean trade. It is possible that the Hawkinses and Drake were distant relations, and the term "cousin", which then was a loose one, is sometimes used. Either because of kinship, or because they recognized some quality in the young man, the Hawkinses took Drake to work for them. By the time he went on the disastrous voyage to San Juan, he had his first command of a ship.

When Drake and Hawkins came home after that dreadful journey, they found that relations with Spain were much worse than when they had left. Religious tension was growing. In France, the Huguenots, or French Protestants, were opposing the Catholic king. In the Netherlands, the Protestant people had risen against the tyranny of their Spanish rulers. Even the ever-cautious Elizabeth had impounded Spanish treasure ships which she believed were carrying money for an invasion of England. A state of what we now call "cold war" existed.

Hawkins was very anxious to go back to the Caribbean to recoup his losses. As he was now the most famous sailor in England, he was ordered to stay at home. The Queen would need him if a shooting war started. Nobody minded, however, if that unknown young man, Francis Drake, went back across the Atlantic for his own vendetta with Spain. That was more or less how he looked on it, on the grounds of both his patriotism and his religious convictions. He bore a strong personal grudge for San Juan de Ulua. Then there were the rumours in Plymouth. Sailors whispered along the water-front that young Drake had been a coward for deserting John Hawkins. Drake was going to stop that story, once and for all.

He sailed from Plymouth late in 1570. He had many complicated schemes, but the purpose behind them was simple. He would capture a consignment of treasure being sent from Peru to Spain.

He spent the next spring on the Isthmus of Panama. Soon he joined up with one of those Frenchmen who for years had been harassing the Spanish in Central America. The man had a great deal to tell him. He made contacts with the Cimaroons, a tribe made up of runaway Negro slaves and the native women. He learnt that all the treasure from Peru which came into Panama was shipped out from one port. This was called Nombre de Dios, or Name of God. Drake asked endless questions about the place. He never learnt to write very fluently, but he could draw a map. He sketched away, to print the plan of the town on his mind, until he felt he could find his way all around it.

He also established a secret harbour. It was a sheltered bay, with only a narrow inlet, so that ships passing by at sea could not peer in. Trees hid it from view from the land. There was a stream of fresh water, and a beach firm and wide enough for boat builders to work. Drake called his harbour Port Pheasant, and buried his surplus stores there to keep for his next expedition.

He spent the winter in Plymouth, then sailed again in 1572. His larger ship, the *Pasco*, belonged to John Hawkins. The other was called the *Swan*. He took seventy-three men with him, including two of his brothers. At twenty-nine or so, Drake himself was almost the oldest man on the expedition. Sailors seldom lived long.

They sailed for Port Pheasant but found that it was no longer a secret. A message nailed to a tree trunk by John Garrett of Plymouth explained to them what had happened. The Spaniards had found the port and dug up the stores. The secret had been betrayed by a Spanish prisoner, whom Drake had captured and then released the previous year. In spite of this, Drake went on being merciful to prisoners all through his career, to a degree that was very rare in his time.

Drake had a log stockade built round the landward side of the port, to defend it against attack. Then he went on with his original plan. He had brought ready-cut and shaped timbers from Plymouth with which he could build pinnaces, or light boats. With these, his men could row silently right into the harbours and take everyone by surprise.

When all was ready, they sailed to the Isle of Pines, which was to be their advanced base. They rowed into Nombre de Dios on a quiet, windless night with a feeble moon. Then they split into two, and attacked on two sides at once. The Spaniards were taken utterly by surprise. All they could do was to fire a few shots, which seemed to do little damage. Now all Drake's work in learning the plan of the town paid off. Although he had never been there before, he was able to lead his men straight to the treasure house. Then came disappointment. They found a store of silver, but no gold. After so much planning, Drake wanted gold. Suddenly, a violent, tropical storm broke out. The English had to huddle in shelter to keep their weapons dry. Then, to their horror, Drake collapsed. Unknown to anyone but himself, he had been shot in the leg and had been losing blood ever since. His men had only one thought; to carry him to the boats. They escaped just as dawn was breaking.

Months of careful scheming had come to nothing.

There was so much thought behind it that many people have said it was John Hawkins who made the plans. Such care was typical of him. Now, Drake was on his own in an enemy country. He would have to improvise plans; and that was what suited his nature.

Drake headed towards the Spanish Main, to give the impression that he had left Panama. Then he doubled back. He deliberately scuttled the *Swan* to leave men free for the more useful pinnaces. He could find another ship later. Once again, he had a clear, basic aim. If he could not capture the Spanish treasure at Nombre de Dios itself, he would seize the next consignment before it got there.

The Cimaroons told him what route the treasure would take. It was landed on the south coast of Panama near Panama City. It was then carried across the Isthmus, the narrowest point in all the American continent, to Nombre de Dios. It would not come for several more months, until the rainy season was over.

The long wait, and the tropical rains, were a test of Drake's driving enthusiasm. He kept his men busy by using the pinnaces for raids on the Spanish Main. A number of men died of fever, including one of his brothers. His other brother was killed by the Spaniards. At last, the Cimaroons brought the news he wanted. The fleet which would carry the treasure to Spain had put in to Nombre de Dios. It would wait there until all the year's consignment of treasure was brought across from Panama in the south. Drake set out through the wild, densely forested country. He took with him eighteen Englishmen, and rather more than that number of Cimaroons. The Cimaroons proved to be expert guides. When they reached the crest of the mountains that form the backbone of Panama, they showed him an enormous tree. There were notches carved deep in the trunk, and Drake started to climb it with them. After a bit, he paused. If he glanced back he could see the Atlantic stretching away. England was somewhere thousands of miles in the distance. He peered through the leaves and branches. Then suddenly, he saw the distant glint of water ahead. He was seeing two different oceans at once. This then was the Pacific, which no Englishman had ever set eyes on before. In that one moment, the whole world expanded and became larger. Drake prayed to God that he might live to sail an English ship on those waters. When he came down, he sent John Oxenham of Plymouth up the tree. Oxenham made the same prayer.

They made their way to the city of Panama. One brave Cimaroon risked going right into the city. He learnt that a mule train, laden with treasure, would leave there the following night. Drake planned an ambush. His men all wore their white shirts outside their coats, so that they could recognize one another in the deep gloom. They crouched down beside the track, waiting. At last, the faint chime of mule bells mingled with the other sounds of the tropical night. It grew louder. Then there was another noise: horse's hooves. A lone Spanish rider approached them. He was coming to meet the convoy. One of the Englishmen, who had been drinking spirits from a flask to keep up his courage, stood up to see who it was. His companions pulled him down quickly. The horseman rode on. He gave no sign of having noticed. With any luck, the alarm was over.

Soon the mule bells came near. Drake commanded his men to attack. But the mules they captured were laden only with baggage. The horseman had given a warning, and the Spaniards had kept all the mules with treasure behind. His second attempt, and he was unlucky again. He marched back to the Atlantic, to join the rest of his men.

Drake would not give up. He joined forces with a French Protestant captain who had come to the Caribbean on the same errand as himself. They agreed that further consignments of gold would be brought to Nombre de Dios. They rowed to a spot some twenty miles from the town. Drake sent his pinnaces away, lest they should be spotted by Spanish patrol boats. He ordered them to come back to the same place in four days' time. Then the Cimaroons guided them to a good spot for an ambush. They hid themselves by the road near the outskirts of Nombre de Dios. The air was still. They could hear the hammer of shipwrights repairing the treasure fleet in the harbour. Children shouted at play. Cocks crowed. At last there came the noise that they wanted, the jangle of mule trains approaching.

This time, there was no mistake. They fell on the Spanish soldiers escorting the treasure. Although the parties were equal in number, there was only a short, sharp fight. The soldiers fled. Drake's men scooped up all the gold they could carry. There was so much that they buried some, along with all the silver. Then they heard shouts. The soldiers had raised the alarm, and the inhabitants of Nombre de Dios were pouring out of the town. They must not stay. They all scattered, except for two of the French party, who stayed behind with their captain who had been wounded. They struggled through dense forest to get back to their rendezvous where the pinnaces would be waiting. When they arrived, there was no one there.

They had no means of escape. Soon, the Spaniards would send out their own boats to search all along the coast. The men, alarmed and indignant, asked one another what could have happened.

Drake thought that the answer was in the wind. It was blowing so hard off-shore that the rescue party must have despaired of having to row against it. There was no time to waste. Shouting out orders as he began to work, he got his men to take logs and lash them into a rough raft. He made a sail of sorts out of biscuit sacks. Another log would do as an oar and rudder combined. They pushed the raft into the water and Drake clambered on to it. An Englishman and two Frenchmen followed.

The wind caught the make-shift sail, and bore them along, over the turbulent sea. Again and again, they had to cling on for their lives as the waves poured over the raft. They wallowed and pitched for hours before they saw their own fleet. Drake was stimulated by all he had been through. He greeted his men with jokes, and the promise of treasure. Then, when he might have wanted to rest, he had to urge a new effort. They must row right into the teeth of the wind to rescue their companions. It took sheer, brute strength on the part of the men, and intense will-power from Drake to encourage them to keep going.

They reached the shore and found everyone safe. Oxenham had gone back to the scene of the ambush. When he returned, he reported that the French captain was dead, and that the Spaniards had dug up the hastily buried treasure. They rowed back to join the fleet.

There was to be no crawling home, as from San Juan de Ulua. Drake sailed back to England in a captured Spanish frigate. He bedecked her with silken streamers and ensigns, and flew the cross of St George. He always had a liking for splendid gestures. The ships carried gold as ballast, worth over a million in modern money. The French were to have their share, and most of the rest would go to the Queen. Even so, Drake would be rich and famous.

His crew would remember him as a battered young man, encrusted with salt and blistered raw by the sun, who had brought his men out of Nombre de Dios by nothing but will-power and courage.

They reached Plymouth one Sunday morning. The townspeople were in St Andrew's, listening to the preacher. Then somebody opened the heavy church

door and called out the news that Drake's ship was coming in. Within minutes, the crowd was jostling and
struggling to get outside. They hurried down the cobbled
streets to the harbour, and ran to the waterside, shouting
and waving. The preacher was left on his own.

6

Round the World

DRAKE'S only fault was that he had been too successful. The Queen was now hoping for better relations with Spain. She arranged that he should disappear quietly for a couple of years. Meanwhile, another Westcountryman appeared on the scene: Richard Grenville of Buckland Abbey near Plymouth.

The Grenvilles were a leading Westcountry family, and Buckland Abbey was one of the finest houses near Plymouth. Grenville secretly looked on the Hawkinses as mere tradesmen, and, not so secretly, thought that Drake was an upstart. Ironically, he was rather like Drake as a person. Both had violent feelings and strongly held opinions. John Hawkins was a more balanced and moderate man than either. When Grenville began to take an interest in adventures across the Atlantic, it meant that voyaging had become socially respectable. Courtiers and university men were now going to play their part.

Grenville's schemes were ambitious. At that time, it was widely believed that there was an unexplored continent in the South Pacific, between America and the Far East. It was given the name of Terra Australis Incognita, the Unknown Land in the South. Many people imagined that it would prove as rich as Peru or China.

Grenville wanted to sail into the Pacific through the Straits of Magellan. The Straits, near the tip of South

America, were the only known way from the Atlantic to the Pacific. They had been discovered, nearly sixty years earlier, by the great Portuguese seaman, Magellan, who had headed the only expedition ever to sail round the world. Grenville planned to discover Terra Australis and take possession of it for England. It would become the English equivalent of the Spanish lands in America. Grenville was one of the first men to see that the future lay with colonization, not merely with trade and plunder.

Once more, the Queen said no. Her intelligence services told her that Spanish ports on the Pacific coast of South America were not guarded. Let a hot-headed man like Grenville loose in the Pacific, and there might be serious trouble. So Drake and Grenville both kicked their heels, while the Queen plotted chances of peace.

Meanwhile, John Oxenham, Drake's old companion, sneaked quietly off from Plymouth. He was not important enough for the Queen to bother about. His plan was to join with the Cimaroons and capture the treasure route across Panama. If he succeeded, the English would have control of the shortest way to the Pacific. He had only fifty Englishmen with him but, as they reminded one another, the Spaniards had captured Central America with tiny armies.

He very nearly succeeded. At one time, he captured more treasure than Drake had ever taken at Nombre de Dios. Then he disappeared. It was a long time before stories about him came back to England. Some people said that a beautiful lady betrayed him to the Spanish authorities. Another story had an alarming ring of truth. He was hiding in jungle country and the Spaniards were looking for him. They came to a place where a river branched into three. They did not know which branch to follow until they saw feathers floating down one of the streams. Oxenham's men had been plucking chickens, and carelessly tossed the feathers away.

Slowly the see-saw of relations with Spain tilted the other way. The Queen plotted and schemed with that tireless brain that was hidden behind the painted mask of her face. If chances of peace were less anyhow, there might be no harm in looking for Terra Australis. She would give an English captain a licence to go through the Straits of Magellan into the Pacific. Should it be Richard Grenville? Long conversations took place in closed, candle-lit rooms. Even the Queen's highest ministers were not allowed to know what was in her mind. She was rumoured to be consulting the men who actually knew about voyages to America; the Hawkins brothers of Plymouth. Gradually news seeped out. The Queen would sponsor an ambitious voyage. Officially, it was intended to go to the Middle East. John Hawkins was busy preparing detailed instructions for trading with Egypt. But, as a few important people were told, it was really to look for Terra Australis. The man in charge would be not Grenville, but Francis Drake.

Had John Hawkins persuaded the Queen that it needed a brilliant navigator to sail through the Straits of Magellan? Or did Elizabeth think that, if the worst came to the worst, it was easier to disown the farmer's son than a Grenville of Buckland Abbey? "The gentleman careth not if I disavow him," she said, and twisted her long, slender fingers.

In 1577, the expedition left Plymouth. The Hawkins interest was represented by Drake's flagship, the *Pelican*, and by young William Hawkins the third. They had to return to Plymouth to repair damage done in gales, and finally they got away in December. Instead of turning into the Mediterranean, as most of the crew had expected, they sailed on into the Atlantic. They stopped at the Cape Verde Islands, where they refreshed themselves on coconut juice, then headed towards the southern part of the South American coast.

So far as the men knew, no English ship had sailed across the Equator before. The ship's chaplain, Fletcher, repeated stories that the climate would be so hot that they would frizzle to death. Amazingly, they survived. What they had not expected was the region known as the Doldrums. There was almost no wind there to move the ships along. As they drifted, Fletcher looked down from the deck of the ship, and saw flying fish hatch out. They scudded about on the water, no bigger than gnats. The sea was a mass of floating jellies with sea serpents swimming about. Some were green, some black, some yellow and some white. Others were all the hues of the rainbow. The sailors rigged up awnings to shelter themselves from the sun. They murmured anxiously. Was this calm caused by witchcraft?

After sixty-three days out of sight of land, they reached the shores of Brazil in South America. They made their way down the coast. At one place where they called in, the inhabitants seemed giants compared to themselves. At another place, an excited native snatched Drake's cap off his head, and wore it himself.

The muttering and the discontent grew. Nobody knew where they were going. Some had been told as a secret that they were looking for Terra Australis. Was this true, or was it a cover for yet a third scheme?

The weather made matters worse. The further south they sailed, the worse it became. It was August, but it might as well have been winter. They had not realized that the seasons would be in reverse in the southern hemisphere. The gales were so bad that it might be weeks before they would be able to enter the Straits of Magellan.

It looked as if the unrest would come to a head as a mutiny against Drake. Not only the seamen were discontented, but the gentlemen who had come with the expedition. According to the ideas of the day, nobody gave orders to his own social equals, and still less to his superiors. Yet here was this semi-illiterate rough-neck who claimed that his word was law, and that everyone must obey him, solely because he was captain. Who did he think he was?

Drake pounced. The chief focus of all the rumours and discontent was a gentleman named Thomas Doughty. He had Doughty executed. He urged his expedition to act together, regardless of all the social distinctions that mattered so much on land. "I must have the gentleman to haul and draw with the mariner, and the mariner with the gentleman." He said they would forget the unhappy things that had happened on board the *Pelican*, and he renamed her the *Golden Hind*. This was a compliment to the courtier, Sir Christopher Hatton, who had a golden hind as his crest. Then he let everyone into the secret. The Queen had given permission for them to raid the unguarded west coast of South America. They might hope to seize more Spanish treasure than anyone had before.

By acting boldly, Drake had made his authority clear. He had brought a new principle into the English Navy; that at sea the captain has absolute charge of his ship and all on board must obey him. By one of the strange coincidences of history, it was at this same spot that Magellan had faced and quelled mutiny fifty-eight years before.

The expedition entered Magellan's Straits. They were narrow and winding, with mountains rising steeply out of the water. The wind gusted and veered fiercely, and the rocky slopes of the mountains were covered with snow and ice. The sailors shot some of the penguins which lived in the Straits. They provided fresh food of a sort, but were very fatty, and tasted strongly of fish.

Drake had Magellan's own charts to help him. By a mixture of luck and skill, he made his way through the

Straits in sixteen days. Magellan himself had taken twice as long. The next men to make the journey, Cavendish, and Richard Hawkins who both sailed from Plymouth, were to take longer still.

Now Drake was in the Pacific at last. He met violent gales, and was driven southwards. Drake, as ever, was stimulated by danger. Once he "cast himself upon the uttermost point" and cried that he was further south than any man in the history of the world. At the same time, his seaman's instincts were hard at work. If the map-makers were right, they should by now have been blown on to Terra Australis. But were they right; those men in London and Oxford who had never once been to sea? The maps put Terra Australis somewhere south of Magellan's Straits. Drake was now almost certain that there was nothing there but sea. This meant South America came down to a point, and you could sail right round it from the Atlantic to the Pacific. Nobody had realized this before. Drake decided to keep very quiet in case the knowledge should help the Spaniards. He would tell a few reliable people like the Hawkinses, when he got home.

In the gales, one ship was lost, and another was blown right back through the Straits. The *Golden Hind* managed to regain her course, and sailed on alone up the west coast of South America. As they went, Drake inquired about Oxenham, his old companion. If Oxenham had been successful, he could sail up to join him. Together they could control the whole Isthmus of Panama. But the story in all the ports was that Oxenham had been captured. The Spaniards held him prisoner in Peru.

So all Drake could do was to raid and to capture treasure. Soon he had so much that the crew threw anything worthless overboard in order to make space for it. South America hummed with stories about the daring young Englishman. His name aroused dread, that was

tinged with reluctant respect. One Spanish captain who
had been raided reported, "When our ship was sacked,
no man dared take anything without his orders: he shows
them great favour, but punishes the least fault."

When Drake had all the booty that he could carry, he
had to find a way home. First he sailed right up the
Pacific coast of North America, further north than anybody is known to have been before. Those mapmakers at
home had a theory that there was a "North-West Passage" around or through North America between the
Atlantic and the Pacific; a northern Straits of Magellan
in other words. Nobody had found the Atlantic end.
After hunting for the Pacific end, Drake's view of the
geography experts was not very greatly improved.

Drake sailed south to what is now California. The
Spaniards had not yet got there, so he could safely put in
to repair his ship. He found the natives were friendly,
almost tiresomely so. A great deal of time was taken up
with ceremonial singing, dancing, and speech making.
Drake decided to hold a ceremony of his own. He named
the place Nova, that is New, Albion, and claimed it for
the Queen. Then he set up a brass plate, which may well
be the same one that was found near San Francisco in
1936. There is a replica in Buckland Abbey, near
Plymouth.

Drake still had to find his way home. The Spaniards
would be expecting him to go back the way he had come,
and would be lying in wait for him. He was not especially
anxious to go through the Straits again. Among the
things he had captured were some charts of the Pacific.
Drake knew that only one expedition in history had ever
sailed right round the world. That was Magellan's,
sixty years earlier. Magellan himself had not lived to come
home. So no captain had ever sailed his own ship round
the world. Drake's lively, expressive face lit up at the
thought of this new challenge.

If John Hawkins had been there, he could have pointed out all the practical problems. The *Golden Hind* was tiny. No record of her exact size exists, and the estimates disagree. To give a rough idea: a tennis court is seventy-eight feet long, and twenty-seven feet wide as used for a game of singles. The *Golden Hind* was probably about ten feet shorter, and ten feet less in the beam at her widest part. Yet her rigging was so complicated that she needed a crew of well over fifty men to handle her, taking turns with the watch. At the other extreme, Francis Chichester, thanks to modern rigging and a self-steering gear, could sail a boat fifty-three feet in length around the world single-handed.

Chichester's boat, *Gipsy Moth IV*, is on view at Greenwich. Anybody who sees her can try to imagine a crew of more than fifty men crammed into a ship that was deeper in the water but not really so very much larger.

This then was Drake's first problem: a tiny ship and a big crew. With such overcrowding, diseases spread very rapidly. Some captains, like John Hawkins and his son Richard after him, used to struggle to keep their crews healthy. They insisted on strict cleanliness; of the ship, of the men, of their clothes. Even so, when diseases once got on board, there were no drugs able to stop them.

Drake's next problem was the constant sense of rottenness and decay. All wooden ships rotted. Worms literally ate them up, especially in warm, tropical waters. Inside the ships, food went bad. Biscuits had maggots crawling in them. Beer and water went rancid. Fish and meat, called "salt horse", were pickled in brine to preserve them, dut were still barely eatable. Rats scuttled everywhere. Cats, poisons and rat traps were powerless to stop them increasing in number.

Most horribly of all, the men's own bodies decayed. Many of them became drowsy and very thirsty, but lost all desire to eat. Their legs swelled up, as did their gums, and their teeth dropped out. It was a disease called scurvy, and, at this time, a thousand English seamen were dying of it every year.

There were other difficulties. Nobody knew just how wide the Pacific was. There were no scientific aids to finding the way. A sensible man might have hesitated. Drake was never a sensible man, but had moments of divine madness. He set out across the Pacific.

They had "nothing in our view but air and sea, without sight of any land for the space of full sixty-eight days together". It is hard nowadays to imagine their absolute isolation. The crew of a space ship in radio contact with earth is not as alone as they were. And the crew of the space ship have more idea where they are going.

At last, they saw land again. Drake had survived the difficulties of a long ocean voyage. He had more problems ahead. Now he had to thread his ship through the many islands of the East Indies. It was a real test of his skill as a navigator. Only once did he go aground, but that was the most dangerous moment of the whole voyage. It was twenty alarming hours before he managed to float his ship off.

One result of this stage of the journey was that Drake bought cloves from the Moluccas, the headquarters of the spice trade. Up till then, the Portuguese had had a monopoly. In a modest way, this was the beginning of English trade with the Far East.

Still, Drake had to sail right across the Indian Ocean, around the Cape of Good Hope, and all the long way up Africa, and then Europe, into Plymouth. With every mile that he covered his chance increased of becoming the first captain ever to sail round the world. To his crew would belong the honour of being the first Englishmen ever to do so.

It was September, 1580, when they sailed into Plymouth Sound. They had been away nearly three years. The obvious thing was to get out of the wind-tossed waters of the Sound, and into the sheltered anchorage of Sutton Pool. For once, Drake acted with caution. He knew he had been astonishingly, extravagantly successful. Either he would become a national hero, or else be in total disgrace for having upset the Spaniards. Everything depended on the political situation, that was to say, on the Queen.

So Drake sheltered behind a small, rocky island, a little offshore from the Hoe. Its name then was St Nicholas Island, but now it is called Drake's Island. He saw a small fishing boat, and called out to the men in it. They looked up in surprise at his question.

"Is the Queen alive and well?"

7

The Dragon

ALL was well.

Drake's loot was put, under guard, into Trematon Castle across the Sound from Plymouth. It was a safe and secluded place to keep so much wealth, with its round tower up on a steep mound overlooking a little creek. All around were long grass, and trees. Marsh birds waded in the creek at low tide.

From Trematon, the treasure was taken by strings of pack horses all the way to the Tower of London. The Spaniards, not surprisingly, demanded to have it back. The Queen, with her usual skill in being evasive, kept them talking and waiting until she thought they might be resigned to their loss. Then she went to see Francis Drake on the *Golden Hind*, which had now sailed round to London. She knighted him, and handed the sword to a representative of the French government. Now the French were involved in honouring Drake as well.

Drake found himself both famous and rich. He was tired of gentlemen who looked down on him. He would become a country landowner too. He knew of a fine estate in Devon that was near enough to Plymouth for him to keep in touch with seafaring matters. He sent agents to negotiate for it. They did not give his name. So it was with a shock that Sir Richard Grenville found he had sold Buckland Abbey to his old rival.

Drake's new home was a former monastery, set in a

fold of green hills looking down on the Tavy and Tamar. The house itself is the old abbey church, built of pale grey stone. Grenville kept the tower and skilfully fitted three floor levels into the church itself. Around the house are sloping, green lawns, and huge, spreading yew trees. A short distance away, stands the monks' old tithe barn, one of the finest in England. Buckland Abbey is now a museum. It seems too peaceful and tranquil a place to have contained such an urgent spirit as Drake's.

While Drake was busy being a country gentleman, and being pointed to as the most famous seaman in England, his old companion, John Hawkins, had settled in London. He now held the vital office of Treasurer of the Navy. It was a job for which he was ideally suited. He was an experienced practical seaman; as a merchant he understood money matters; and he was a balanced and thoughtful man well able to plan ahead. During the ten years, 1578–1588, he worked tirelessly at improving the design of English ships and the conditions on board. He was the first to suggest that it would be better to pay sailors more to attract fewer, better men, than to take on large crews of riff-raff. All this was background work, and did not attract public notice. But by 1588, the English Navy owed much more to John Hawkins than to any one other man.

William, the other second generation Hawkins, was still in Plymouth. The two brothers remained in close touch. William was three times Mayor of Plymouth, and sounds a steady, reliable type. Yet William, like his father and brother, showed the dual side of the Hawkins nature. In 1582, when he was sixty-three, he set out on a voyage from Plymouth, and came back with a valuable load of pearls, treasure, hides, and sugar. No one in Plymouth was worried to think that he might have plundered the Spaniards.

It was not until 1585 that the Queen unleashed

Francis Drake, and gave him permission to sail again to the Caribbean. Spain was now stronger than ever. King Philip had inherited the Portuguese throne, and the two countries were united. The Dutch leader, William of Orange, who ranked with Elizabeth as Philip's chief enemy, had been assassinated. None the less, England and Spain were still not officially at war. Elizabeth wanted Drake to annoy the Spanish and to take any treasure he could. She did not want open war.

Drake headed a big expedition. There were two naval vessels and twenty-seven others. The Vice-Admiral was a Yorkshireman, Martin Frobisher. Frobisher was famous for trying to find the Atlantic end of the North-West Passage, for which Drake, too, had sought in vain from the Pacific. Like Drake, he was a brave and determined man. He was also hot tempered, and very outspoken in a rough, violent manner. From the first, he and Drake grated on one another. Lesser men trembled, and kept out of their way.

Drake left Plymouth in a hurry, having some fear that his orders might be cancelled. He did not stop to take on full supplies of water and food, and very soon he ran short. Anyone else would have called in at a friendly, or at least neutral port. Drake, being Drake, put into Vigo in Spain and demanded supplies. Soon, all Europe buzzed with the news. It was not only Drake who thought he was waging a personal war with Spain. The Spaniards thought so too. They forgot that England had many other fine seamen. Instead of saying the English fleet did something, they said Drake did it.

Drake sailed on into the Atlantic, and stopped at the Cape Verde Islands. There his men were attacked by one of their worst enemies, fever. Two thousand three hundred men had left Plymouth. Three hundred of them died in a matter of days. Many more fell ill as they sailed on to Hispaniola. In spite of this, Drake approached the capital city with a great show of force. The garrison prepared to defend it. Meanwhile, Drake sneaked round with a smaller force, and captured it from the rear.

The Caribbean, too, hummed with stories of El Draque, the Dragon. Nurses told frightened children about this wild Englishman who was both more and less than human. The legend grew. Not many people would bother to listen to the balanced view of one Spaniard who had actually seen him. "A man of medium stature, blond, rather heavy than slender, merry, careful. He commands and governs imperiously . . . Sharp, restless, well-spoken, inclined to liberality and to ambition, vainglorious, boastful, not very cruel." "Not very cruel," it was nonsense. Easier to believe that the Dragon had horns and a tail.

From Hispaniola, Drake sailed to Cartagena, the chief city of the Spanish Main. It was heavily fortified. The traditional thing to do would have been to sit down and mount a long siege. Drake made a sudden attack by night. He seized all the big guns of the city in his first swoop, and left it defenceless. Everyone along the coast trembled, wondering where he would pounce next. But a new fever was raging among his men. Drake decided to head for home.

He sailed north up the American coast to get into the Gulf Stream and into the westerly winds that would carry him back to Plymouth. On his way, he called in at the English colony in Virginia that had been established the year before by Sir Richard Grenville. He found the colonists short of food. All their determination and enthusiasm had gone. Drake agreed to evacuate them to England. Unfortunately, Grenville himself arrived with supplies of food less than two weeks later. When he heard what had happened, he had yet another score to add to his grievances against Drake.

As a means of obtaining money, this expedition failed. As a means of "showing the flag" it was an enormous success. In spite of it, rumours still grew that Spain meant to invade England. England must take steps to prevent this, and who could do better than Drake? In spring, 1587, he set out again from Plymouth. The Queen had given permission for him to sail into Spanish ports. Once again, he left in a hurry, for fear that she would cancel his orders. She did so, but the message arrived several days too late. Drake was already at sea. A pinnace was sent out to fetch him, but could not catch him up. The Queen had made a muddle of things, and did not know her own mind. Or did she know perfectly well that by doing this she could have the best of both worlds? She had publicly tried to stop Drake and yet left him free to do whatever he wanted to do in Spain.

For Drake now embarked on the most outrageous exploit of his career. He sailed right into a Spanish port: Cadiz, in the far south of Spain. The townspeople were panic-stricken. The Spaniards fought back by sending in their galleys. These were boats rowed by banks of oars which had been the traditional fighting ships in the Mediterranean ever since classical times. They were no match for the English. The Navy that Hawkins was shaping had fast-moving sailing ships, with big, brass guns.

For a fantastic day and a half, Drake held the Spanish harbour. He fended off attacks from the galleys and from fire ships as well. The Spanish shore guns could not destroy him. For twelve hours of that time, he was becalmed among sand banks, but still they could not get near him. When he sailed out in triumph, he had destroyed about thirty ships. The Spaniards were left to weigh up the damage. Some unfortunate person would have to report the news to King Philip.

Philip's reaction was balanced. "The loss is not very

3. Elizabethan house near Sutton Harbour,
now a museum

City Museum and Art Gallery, Plymouth

Habes Lector candide fortiss. ac inuictiss. Ducis Draeck ad Viuum simaginem qui toto terrarum orbe, duorum annorum, et mensium decem spacio. Zephiris fauentibus circumducto. Angliam sedes proprias. 4. Cal Octobr. anno á partu virginis 1580 reuisit cum antea portu soluisset Id. Decem: anni 1577.

4. Sir Francis Drake by Joss de Hondt

City Museum and Art Gallery, Plymouth

great," he declared, "but the daring of the attempt was very great indeed." He knew, and everyone else in Spain knew, that it all added to the Drake legend.

For the next seven weeks, Drake harried the southern coasts of Spain and Portugal. Everyone trembled as he sailed by, for nothing was safe from him. He burnt fishing boats, even nets. On beach after beach, there were spurts of flame and columns of smoke as he burnt the boats drawn up there. He attacked small trading vessels, and burnt their cargoes of wood. Some people shrugged this off as sheer vindictiveness. Drake, as a practical seaman, knew quite well what he was doing. The wood was the sort that was needed for making barrels. Sound barrels were essential for carrying food and water on board ship. Yet not even Drake saw fully that burning the barrel staves was more serious if less spectacular than what he had done at Cadiz.

Drake had troubles of his own. The Vice-Admiral of the expedition was called Thomas Burroughs. Like Grenville, and Frobisher, and the dead Doughty, Burroughs decided that Drake was an impossible man to get on with. The expedition split up. Drake sailed off towards the Azores. He had heard rumours of a large Portuguese ship homeward-bound from India. Perhaps he could intercept her. He worked out what he knew of the winds and currents and her likely speed. Then he sailed on till he saw the great ship, which towered in the water, high over his own.

Drake's skill in hunting out ships at sea was all a part of his legend. His enemies said that he had a magic mirror down in his cabin. He peered into it, and he could see the movements of all the ships in the world. Drake's crews, who unlike their social superiors, looked on him with near-worship, could have told them the truth. For sheer knowledge of sea-craft, Drake was now without rival in all the world.

3

Drake captured the Portuguese ship. There were not many other captains who had the will to resist when they heard the name "Drake". Being a merciful man at heart, Drake gave the Portuguese a small ship to carry them home. Then he sailed his prize back for another triumphant entry to Plymouth Sound. She was laden with spices, ivories, silks, and gold, and silver, and jewels. Her value was worth more than double the cost of the expedition.

When Drake got home, he said, in a famous phrase, that he had "singed the King of Spain's beard". A singed beard can grow again, and a great invading force might yet sail. But instead of having high hopes, and a certainty of success, it would set out in doubt, and in fear.

8

"Let Tyrants Fear"

IN HIS strange palace of the Escorial, Philip II of Spain brooded on war.

He had had the Escorial built about thirty miles from Madrid, to be remote from the distractions of life in the city. He chose a site among mountains; harsh and bleak in the winter, harsh and barren under the merciless summer sun. It was built to last for ever, with thick granite walls, lined with lead, that would show none of the softening effects of age. Because of Philip's own temperament, the place was half a palace and half a monastery. A church was its centre point, and Philip himself lived and worked obsessively in a tiny room hidden away by the church. It was no bigger and no more comfortable than a monk's cell. Yet as Philip himself said, "I rule the affairs of half the world." It was true, for his empire was now bigger than the Roman Empire had been in its greatest days.

Outside the Escorial, a few men wondered uneasily. Philip spent so much time on his knees, with his eyes fixed on the flickering candles of the high altar. Did he really know what was happening in the world outside?

In England, Elizabeth smiled with her lips, and hooded her heavy eyes to hide what she was thinking. She still hoped to avoid war. For the moment, she would apologize for what one of her ministers called Drake's "indiscreet brags". Meanwhile, John Hawkins worked on. If war really came, he was going to have the English fleet ready. His new ships were the opposite of that wretched *Jesus of Lubeck*. He had had them built longer, so that they were faster and could sail closer to the wind than the old, very wide vessels. He had got rid of those high superstructures that were so troublesome in rough seas. He had tried to make conditions on board fit for good fighting men. Spanish spies heard stories of how all the old diehards opposed him. They did not realize how much he had achieved.

In Plymouth too the English worked tirelessly. The chief base for repairing ships was then the Cattewater, or estuary of the Plym. All through the spring and early summer of 1588, the shipwrights hammered away day and night. Huge, flaming torches were tied on to posts so that they could see to work. Sometimes the winds were so strong that the flames blew dangerously; sometimes the flames were nearly quenched by the driving rain. When he had finished his other duties, the Mayor of Plymouth stumped up and down on the muddy banks, urging the shipwrights on. He went home to find that his wife and her maids were stitching away by candle-light to make flags for the ships. Then he settled down to write a report for the Treasurer of the Navy. The Spaniards did not know the strength of the link between William and John Hawkins.

England's urgent need was now to appoint a commander. Her most famous seaman was Drake. The common sailors idolized him, but would any other captain obey his orders? Grenville certainly would not. That braggart Martin Frobisher was rumoured to have threatened to "spill the best blood in his belly". To avoid trouble, the Lord Admiral, Lord Howard of Effingham, was given command of the fleet. He was not an experienced sailor, but according to the ideas of the day, everyone was expected to obey a man of exalted rank.

Howard sailed down to Plymouth in May 1588. He was ceremonially saluted by Drake, who had become Vice-Admiral of the Fleet. Both men behaved very well. Howard showed great tact and dignity. Drake decided not to exploit his amazing personal magnetism at such a serious moment.

When they met, they did not realize that the Spanish Armada was already at sea.

It was a terrible summer for weather. The Spaniards ruefully told one another that the only difference between the English summer and the English winter was that in summer the days were longer. The English fleet was kept in Plymouth by gales. The south-west winds blew so fiercely that no ships could beat out of the Sound against them. The Cattewater was crammed tight with shipping. Drake took the shelter of St Nicholas Island. Lord Howard was left to ride out the gales in the open Sound, "where we have danced as lustily as the gallantest dancers in court".

While he tossed there, the Spaniards had been driven back to Corunna. They had nearly exhausted their food supplies, and their water barrels were leaking. Drake's burnings on the beaches were starting to have effect.

Back in Corunna, the Spanish commander took stock. He was the Duke of Medina Sidonia, who had been appointed at the last moment when the former commander died. Like Lord Howard, he had high social position and no knowledge of naval affairs. He did not even like sailing. "I know by experience of the little I have been at sea that I am always seasick and always catch cold." In Corunna, he looked at the Spanish fleet from the viewpoint of a sensible, conscientious man. He wrote to Philip suggesting that the Armada should not sail that year. This proves that he was also a brave man, for Philip ruled with absolute power.

While Medina Sidonia was waiting for Philip's reply,

the English fleet sailed out of Plymouth. They hoped to attack the enemy in their own waters, but within a day's sail of the Spanish coast they were driven back by more gales. Then Philip's answer came. Sidonia must refit and sail, with no further argument. He left again on the very day that the English got back to Plymouth. They now flattered themselves that the Spanish Armada could not sail that year. It was a shock when they heard that the fleet had been sighted near the Isles of Scilly, off the far south-west of England.

The men on shore turned towards the sea as if they would hurry on to their ships. Then they stopped. The flood tide was pouring into the Sound with a strong, visible flow. The watchers on shore saw the water swirl past the wooded slopes of Mount Edgecumbe and up by the marshy banks of the Tamar. They measured its flow by the flotsam bobbing about. All the time, the west wind blew keenly towards the land. A few Londoners might imagine that they could sail out of the Sound, but the Plymouth-born seamen knew better. They would have to wait until evening, and use the force of the outgoing tide to carry them out to sea.

As the ships were made ready for sea, the wait began to tell upon the men's nerves. Then the rumour went round that Drake was perfectly calm. He knew that they could not sail yet, so he had gone on playing bowls on the Hoe. A few sceptics wondered if the story was really true, but at least it proved one thing. Drake could do anything, and get away with it.

It was night when the English fleet sailed out past Rame Head to the open sea. On the headland, a beacon burned. Further east, towards London, a small dot of colour showed where the next beacon had just been lit. Beyond it would be another, and then another, all the way along the South Coast. Another beacon burnt on the fringes of Dartmoor, part of a chain that would carry the warning northwards to York and Durham and into the furthermost parts of England.

Dawn came, and the people of Cornwall gathered on cliff-tops to see the two fleets. The Spanish ships were terrifying and magnificent at the same time. They were towering and stately, with high "castles" fore and aft. They sailed in a strict crescent formation, with the tips of the crescent at their rear. Their seamanship and discipline were superb. The English ships, of Hawkins' new Navy, were more nimble and streamlined. Already, under cover of darkness, they had started to manœuvre round to the rear of the Spanish fleet. As the wind was still blowing hard from the west, this meant that they, not the Spaniards, would have the advantage of catching the wind first.

The day was squally and gusty. The splendid flags, with which both fleets were bedecked, drooped with the weight of the rain. The visibility was too poor for the on-lookers to glimpse the bright colours of the ships; red, green, and black and white. At times, the squalls were so fierce that even the seamen could not make out the details of other ships, with their figureheads and carvings of strange beasts. In the blinding rain, still more English ships slipped round to the rear of the Spanish fleet.

Everything was set for an epic battle. Then there was an anti-climax. Nobody was quite certain what to do. The traditional thing was to grapple with the enemy ships and then send your sailors on board for hand-to-hand fighting. This might work all right in Mediter-ranean harbours, but how on earth could you do it in the choppy and wind-tossed waters of the English Channel? Better try the new style of fighting which meant shooting cannon balls at the enemy. Both sides shot. Since the size of the cannon balls varied, as did the amount of powder used by the gunners, the results were spirited rather than accurate. No one but Drake had ever thought of trying target practice, and he had been reprimanded because ammunition was so expensive. The fleets drew apart again. The first two casualties of the campaign then occurred. The gunpowder store on one Spanish ship blew up, giving rise to a whole host of picturesque explanations. A Spanish ship called the *Rosario* collided with another and damaged her bowsprit.

The Armada sailed on past Plymouth. The English congratulated themselves that at least it had not tried to put in there to capture the port. They did not know that Philip had given firm orders that it was to sail right up the Channel to rendezvous with the Spanish armies in the Netherlands. The wind lessened, but the Spanish fleet still sailed on in its unbroken crescent formation. The sight of so many tall ships packed so closely together was awe-inspiring. They moved slowly, at only two or three miles an hour, and in an uncanny silence. To the English, they looked like sleep-walkers, and nobody knew what they would do when they awoke into life.

Night fell once again. The Spaniards went on, almost drifting rather than sailing. They had had to abandon the *Rosario* and her crew. The English fleet followed behind. Lord Howard told Drake to go first in the *Revenge*. He must hang a great lantern over the stern of his ship to guide the rest of the fleet. Suddenly, Howard realized that the lantern was very much further ahead than he would have expected. He put on more sail to catch up. When dawn broke, he found that he and two other ships were far ahead of the rest of the English fleet. Drake had disappeared. It had been a Spanish lantern that they had followed, and they were inside the pincers of the Spanish crescent formation.

The Spaniards were slow on the uptake, and they managed to wriggle free. When Lord Howard saw Drake again, he had a typical Drake story to tell. He had seen some shadowy shapes in the night. He had feared that the Spaniards were trying to double back to get the advantage of the wind from the English fleet. He hurried off in pursuit, and for security reasons he put out his light. Just as he discovered that all he had seen were a few harmless German ships, he happened, by sheer coincidence naturally, to find himself near the *Rosario*. When he told her captain his name, she had surrendered to him. Typical Drake, agreed everybody. Who else would disobey orders to go off on his own affairs? Who else could win such rich prize-money by just shouting out the one syllable of his name?

The Armada continued its slow but majestic course on beyond Torbay. Medina Sidonia did not attempt to land. Off Portland Bill there was another confused battle. Neither side achieved anything. The Spaniards could not get near enough to the English ships to board them, for the English ships were too nimble. Nor could the English break the iron discipline of that unbroken crescent formation. Both sides started to run short of ammunition.

The next engagement took place off the Isle of Wight. The English feared that the Spaniards might land there, or else attempt to seize Portsmouth. Once more, it decided nothing. Drake and John Hawkins tried to drive the Spanish fleet on to the rocks and shoals, but Medina Sidonia realized what was happening, almost at the last moment. The Armada resumed its slow, and it seemed inexorable, progress.

On the deck of his flagship, Lord Howard knighted John Hawkins and Martin Frobisher. Hawkins was very solemn. The English ships were as nimble as he had hoped. Because of this, their guns had inflicted more damage than the Spanish ones had, though their shooting was still wildly inaccurate. But they had not achieved their main object: to stop the Spanish fleet.

Then at last, after all the long-drawn-out days, something decisive happened. Medina Sidonia dropped
anchor off Calais. He was going to wait for Spanish
troops from the Low Countries to join him. He would then
ferry them over to invade England. He had no definite
rendezvous, and did not realize how hopeless the plan
was. The Spanish troops were frightened of Dutch seamen, and would only put out in their little barges if the
Spanish warships came to protect them. But the Spanish
warships were much too big to sail into the shallow
waters where the barges were waiting for them. Philip,
far away in his monk's cell in Spain, had failed to co-
ordinate his plans.

Before Medina Sidonia could resolve his dilemma,
Howard moved.

The new style of battle by guns had proved more or
less inconclusive. So Howard tried an older method of
fighting. Night fell, then a sudden glare appeared in the
darkness, casting a lurid red shadow on to the water
below. The English had sent in their fire-ships.

They had to wait until morning to see what had happened. When light came, they saw that the Spaniards
had scattered at last. One of their largest ships had been
damaged in a collision. The English closed in. The
Spaniards fought back bravely, still trying to grapple and
board their adversaries. It looked as if the English would
at last win a decisive sea battle, if only because they had
more ammunition left. The battle raged until late after-
noon, when a blinding squall of rain stopped it. When
the air cleared, the English could see that the Spanish
fleet was sailing away. Once again, with the gallantry of
despair, they had formed into their crescent moon.

It was the end. The Armada sailed northwards, badly
damaged by the last battle. They dared not put back into
the English Channel, for they had no shot left. They were
short of food, and, thanks to Drake's work on the barrels,

their water supplies were rotting in unseasoned casks. They had to make a long journey home, round the far north of Scotland and all round Ireland. Many ships, already damaged by English gunfire, were wrecked by violent storms. Men died of fever or lack of food. It was a wretched, demoralized remnant of the proud fleet that limped home.

All was not well with the English fleet either. Their sailors, too, were suffering from sickness and lack of food. It took such a short time for shipboard conditions to affect the men's health. The chief sailors felt that the whole episode of the Armada had been inconclusive. They had failed to administer a crushing defeat.

It was left to somebody not a sailor at all to show what the Armada meant. Elizabeth went to review her forces at Tilbury. It was an age when kings and queens were assassinated, but she chose as her protection only four men and two boys. She said, "I do not desire to live to distrust my faithful and loving people. Let tyrants fear. I have always so behaved myself that, under God, I have placed my chiefest strength and safeguard in the loyal hearts and good will of my subjects." When she knew that she had their sympathy and attention she went on. "I know I have the body of a weak and feeble woman, but I have the heart and stomach of a king, and a king of England too, and think foul scorn that Parma or Spain, or any prince of Europe should dare to invade the borders of my realm; to which, rather than any dishonour shall grow by me, I myself will take up arms, I myself will be your general, judge, and rewarder of every one of your virtues in the field."

As so often, this brilliant, maddening woman showed a superlative sense of occasion. She summed up the mood of a confident England who had learnt that it could stand up to Spain. Fifty years before, when old William Hawkins had first sailed out of Plymouth, England had been an obscure off-shore island, and Spain the mightiest country in the world. From the moment Howard led his fleet out of Plymouth to meet the Armada, the balance was starting to tilt in the other direction.

9

The Drum

IN NOVEMBER, 1595, John Hawkins died off
Puerto Rico. His death was a sad one. At that time,
his son Richard was a prisoner of the Spaniards in Peru.
After many years, he was to come home, and win fame
as the third generation of seafaring Hawkinses. His
father was never to know this.

Hawkins died, too, on bad terms with Drake, who was
joint commander on the voyage. The difference in
temperament between the two men had led to a quarrel
about how their ships should be provisioned. Hawkins'
love of careful planning and of arranging his schemes in
detail, contrasted unhappily with Drake's improvisation
and snatching at all opportunities as they offered.

Hawkins has left curiously little memorial. He was one
of the great architects of the English Navy, whom his
country has largely forgotten. In a city that owes more to
the Hawkins family than to any one other family in its
history, there is no street that bears their name.

Two months later, Drake died on the same voyage.
Like Hawkins, he too was not fated to die in a moment of
glory. Drake's life in the past few years had not matched
his splendid stretch of achievement between the raid on
Nombre de Dios and the Armada. He had sailed from
Plymouth against the Spaniards in 1589, but the expedition had ended in failure. After that, he was forced to
vegetate, and to occupy himself with local affairs in

Devon. His main achievement during those years was to bring the waters of the River Meavy to Plymouth to be the town's water supply. It was carried in a stone channel, like a miniature canal. This can still be seen snaking over Roborough Down today, and is still known as "Drake's leat".

In dying, Drake returned to his former self. Before he died, he asked to be dressed in his armour, to meet death like a warrior. He was buried at sea, nobody knows just where.

Drake died, and his drum was brought back to England. It was made of wood, painted red, with a coat of arms on one side. With it came the story that if England was ever in danger, the drum should be struck, and Drake himself would return.

Drake's drum is kept in Buckland Abbey today. Thousands of people go every year to see it. It has become, over the years, a precious possession of the whole English people.

It could be that too much fuss has always been made about Drake. He was only one among many other fine seafarers of his day. His faults were as glaring and obvious as his courage. Yet to England's enemies he, more than anyone, even the Queen, became the living symbol of England. He had some power to weave spells over men's minds, and this stretches down through the centuries, embodied in the fragile shape of his drum.

Francis Drake in his lifetime, and four hundred years later, was two distinct things at once. On the factual level, he was a brilliant but tiresome seaman. On another, perhaps truer level, he is among the immortal heroes of legend.

PART II

THE NEW WORLD

"The name of the Lord is a strong tower."
The Book of Proverbs, and origin of
the motto of the City of Plymouth.

10

New Found Land

GREAT changes do not always take place dramatically.

On the face of it, the future lay with men like
Hawkins and Drake as they sailed out of Plymouth with
all their dreams of conquest and gold. But already the
balance was changing, and new ideas entering in.

The urge to sail to America had begun in the cities. It
had started down on the quaysides, and in crowded
streets of tall houses where rich merchants lived. In the
far south-west of England, Plymouth had taken the lead.
There was a sense of excitement in the air, as shown in
the moment when everyone went rushing out of St
Andrew's to meet Drake.

News of what was happening in Plymouth spread to
other parts of the west. It was carried along the deep,
narrow Devon lanes to manor houses hidden in lush,
wooded valleys. The men and boys who lived there
strolled by their inland streams and talked of America for
the first time. If so much was to be discovered there,
should it all be left to those merchants in Plymouth?
Someone, more realistic than the others, pointed out
that very few West Country gentlemen had as much solid
money behind them as the Hawkinses must have. Even
so, said another, there was more than gold in America.
He looked round his own spreading acres. In America,
there was land.

The gentlemen's sons who talked in this way were a different breed from Drake and the Hawkinses. Drake and John Hawkins had both risen high in society, but, at heart, they were practical seamen. As boys, they had had their hands blistered raw by wet ropes. They had fought to hold the long tillers, which were still used for steering, while their ships bucked under their feet. The sailors who so adored Drake knew quite well that, in a crisis, he could undertake any one of their tasks for them. By contrast, the country land-owners' sons had been to Oxford, or to the Inns of Court. They were friendly with scholars and poets. If they had fought, it was as soldiers in foreign wars, not at sea. Some had been at court, and served the Queen herself. When they were at home, their interest was in their estates. So, when they talked of America, they did not think in terms of adventure at sea. They talked of owning more land, and of settling new communities there.

The leaders in this came from a small, tightly-knit group of kinsmen. Two of them were half-brothers. Their mother, Elizabeth Champernowne, was the sister of Sir Arthur Champernowne, Vice-Admiral of the West. She married first Otto Gilbert who lived by the river Dart, and had three sons: John, Humphrey, and Adrian. After he died, she married Walter Ralegh, who lived near the Exe estuary. She had a son, also called Walter. She must have been a very remarkable woman, for all her sons were men of note in their day. Two of them, Humphrey Gilbert and Walter Ralegh, were responsible for the first real links between England and North America. In this they were joined by another kinsman, Richard Grenville of Buckland Abbey. He was related to them, through the Champernownes, by several family marriages.

This new group of men were well educated, unlike Drake who never learnt to write grammatical English.

They were used to expressing opinions, and wrote "Discourses" explaining their vision of what America could become. They were friendly with men like the clergyman, Richard Hakluyt, that great chronicler and inspirer of voyages.

They began to look to new parts of the American continent. Drake and the Hawkinses had centred their interests on the Caribbean. Their route to America was the one that Columbus had followed. They sailed down the African coast, and then let the winds blow them over to Hispaniola. This region would obviously be hopeless for settlement, because the Spaniards were in complete control. So Humphrey Gilbert, the first of the group to take an active interest in America, fixed his thoughts further north. The obvious place was the one part of North America already known. It was the nearest point of the continent to England, and had been discovered by John Cabot in 1497. It was known as the New Found Land. Since Cabot's time, it had been inhabited for a few months' each summer by fishermen, who dried and salted their catch of codfish before bringing it back to Europe. The other advantage of going north was that they might even discover a North West Passage to China.

It was in 1578 that Humphrey Gilbert was granted a patent to colonize. This was permission to found a colony in America. He might go anywhere provided it was north of Florida. The Spaniards had now established control up as far as Florida, and the Queen was very determined to keep out of their way. In the same year, Gilbert sent out his first expedition from the Isle of Wight. In Hakluyt's words it "began, continued, and ended adversely".

Two years later, Drake returned from his voyage round the world. He was the most discussed man in Europe. When so much money was to be got from plunder, it was hard to raise any interest in new schemes for colonies. It looked as if Gilbert's plans would come to nothing for lack of support. He had to beg round for money. He even sold plots of land in an empire that only existed in his dreams.

At last, he had enough money. His young half-brother, Walter Ralegh, helped. Ralegh was now at Court, and becoming a great favourite with the Queen. He contributed a ship called the *Bark Ralegh*. But as Gilbert got enough money, time began to run out. By 1583, his patent had only one more year left. He assembled his expedition in Cawsand Bay, across the Sound from Plymouth. They were delayed in starting. This meant, as so often happened in those days, that the men ate much of their food before they even set sail.

When they started, nothing went smoothly. The *Bark Ralegh*, their biggest ship, deserted two days out of Plymouth. On their way across to Newfoundland, the weather was very foggy. It was hard for the ships to keep contact with one another. To make matters worse, they had to split up every night to avoid the risk of collisions. Once, one ship, the *Swallow*, was feared lost. She finally reappeared, and all her men had new clothes. They had been indulging in piracy.

Their first glimpse of land, which was probably Labrador, they found unattractive. They landed in Newfoundland early in August. Gilbert was cheered by the sight of the country. It was largely covered by forest; spruce, fir, aspen, and birch, with whortleberries and wild roses. "The country being very good and full of all sorts of victual," he wrote hopefully. Another man on the expedition was meanwhile writing a different sort of letter. "What shall I say, my good Hakluyt, when I see nothing but a very wilderness?"

Wilderness or not, they found the harbour inhabited by some three hundred fishermen. As well as the English, there were French, Spanish, and Portuguese. They were all there for curing their catch. Gilbert's arrival made a welcome break in their somewhat monotonous summer. In August, 1583, Gilbert had a sod of earth cut, and formally took possession of Newfoundland. Drake's claiming of Nova Albion four years before had never been followed up, so Newfoundland therefore became the first part of North America to belong to the English crown. It remained an English colony from that time, until it became a part of the Dominion of Canada in 1949.

Seventeen days later, they sailed southwards. They hoped to run into warmer weather before autumn came. Unluckily, Gilbert was not an experienced naval commander. The Queen herself had called him "a man of no good hap by sea." His men began to doubt if he really knew what he was doing.

The *Swallow* was sent back to England with the inevitable sick men on board. After that, luck ran out fast. Discipline became bad, and they tempted fate by overloading their ships. The biggest was wrecked on a sandbank, and most of her men were drowned. She had been laden with samples of what Gilbert hoped was precious metal, dug up in Newfoundland. The men on the two remaining ships begged him to turn back.

Gilbert would not listen. He stayed on the tiny ship, *Squirrel*, which he had bought for exploring harbours and creeks on the coast. The wind was violent, and the ships rushed down into deep hollows between the waves. Above them, the crested waves towered, looking as high and solid as white cliffs in the murky gloom. Once a mysterious beast passed close by one of the ships, "yawning and gaping wide, with ugly demonstration of long teeth and glaring eyes . . . he sent forth a horrible voice roaring or bellowing as doth a lion." It might have been a walrus; it might, the terrified sailors thought, be a warning of some dreadful fate.

North of the Azores, the storms became more fierce than ever. The men in the larger ship peered anxiously at the tiny *Squirrel*. When they came within hailing distance, they could see that Gilbert was sitting on deck reading, as if to prove that he was not worried. He waved and shouted to them, "We are as near to heaven by sea as by land."

It grew dark, and lights went on in the little ship. Suddenly, the lights disappeared. The onlookers thought that she was down in the trough of a very deep wave. They waited, becoming more anxious as each minute passed. She was never seen again.

Gilbert died with little solid achievement to show. What he did do was to make a beginning in something of immeasurable importance, the settlement of North America by English-speaking people.

I I

"Stars Must Fall"

ON GILBERT'S death, his patent was given to
his young brother, Walter Ralegh. It gave him
permission "to discover, search, find out, and
view such remote heathen and barbarous lands, countries
and territories, not actually possessed of any Christian
prince, nor inhabited by Christian people."

Ralegh had already come far. By London standards,
he was no more than the son of a small landowner in a
remote part of the country. He kept a broad Devonshire
accent all through his life. But he was a talented man,
who had obvious personal fascination. He played a
prominent part at Court, and was a great favourite of the
Queen. He was a scholar, who later wrote a history of the
world. If he had done nothing else, he would still be
remembered nowadays as an accomplished poet. So it
was a brilliant and complex mind that was now turned
to the problems of trying to found settlements in America.

Ralegh was not able to go there himself. For most of
his life he was either too much in favour at Court, or too
much out of favour, to have any real freedom of movement. Instead, he organized two ships to go on a recon-
naissance expedition. The captains were Arthur Barlow,
and Philip Amadas of Plymouth. Amadas was connected
with the Hawkinses by marriage.

The ships left a West Country port, almost certainly
Plymouth, in April, 1584. They took the now usual route

77

across to the West Indies, then sailed northwards up the American coast until they were safely out of the area where the Spanish had settled. They headed for shore in what is now Carolina. Barlow stood on deck in a state of enchantment. "The second of July we found shoal water, where we smelt so sweet and so strong a smell, as if we had been in the midst of some delicate garden abounding with all kinds of odiferous flowers, by which we were assured that the land could not be far distant." His mood lasted when they landed, and the natives of the place came hurrying up towards them, delighted to see these strange, light-skinned men. "We found the people most gentle, loving and faithful, void of all guile and treason, and such as live after the manner of the golden age." Two of the Indians sailed back with them when they left, and one, Manteo, was to remain a loyal friend.

When they returned, Barlow and Amadas reported their findings to Ralegh. The new land was named Virginia, in compliment to the virgin Queen. The term covered not only the modern Virginia, but Georgia and the Carolinas as well. Ralegh decided that it would be a promising region for sending out settlers. It sounded more fertile than Newfoundland, and had a much pleasanter climate. Ralegh had long discussions with Hakluyt about what he should do next.

He was still not free to go out himself, so he chose as leader of the next expedition his kinsman, Sir Richard Grenville. Grenville was a man of violent feelings, less complex and varied than Ralegh. He was well suited to head the expedition, for he had been one of the first men to suggest that England should found colonies overseas. As captains did not then have to know how to sail a ship, Amadas was in charge of the naval side of affairs. One of the ships was commanded by Thomas Cavendish, who later became the third man to sail round the world.

Because Ralegh was a thoughtful man, who was in-

terested in science, he also asked Thomas Hariot to go
out to Virginia. Hariot later became the greatest English
mathematician and astronomer of his time. Much of his
work was connected with seafaring. He helped navigators
by improving their instruments, by fixing the true position of the Pole Star, and by showing them how to allow
for the curve of the earth's surface. He helped start a very
important tradition whereby exploration and scientific
discovery are linked together. Another of the gifted
crew was John White. He was perhaps the first English
painter in water-colours, and certainly the first to make
paintings of the New World.

They left Plymouth in April, 1585. Once again, they
took the route to the West Indies and then northwards.
They landed among the low-lying islands of the Virginia
coast. Once again, the Indians seemed to be friendly.
When they sailed for home in August, they left a hundred
and seven men behind them on Roanoke Island. Ralph
Lane was in command. The first English colony had
been founded.

Within a few weeks, the flaws in the scheme became
alarmingly clear. It was too late in the year for the
colonists to plant any crops of their own. They had
planned to live off the friendly and hospitable Indians.
As winter came near, and food was more scarce, the
Indians were not friendly and hospitable any longer.
They were understandably annoyed that the colonists
would not even fish for themselves. Unfortunately, most
of the men were soldiers and adventurers. What were
really needed were farmers and master craftsmen. They
sat down, passively, to wait until Grenville came back
with fresh food supplies.

A fleet arrived in June, 1586. It was not Grenville, but
Drake, on his way home from raiding Spanish colonies in
the Caribbean. As already told, Drake took the English
colonists back home with him. When Grenville arrived

less than two weeks later and found out what had happened, he blamed not the colonists but Drake. He left a small party of fifteen men behind before he sailed away to work off his bad temper by raiding in the Azores.

This short-lived colony had two far-reaching effects. It proved that it was possible for a party of Englishmen to live nearly a whole year in America. The colonists had learnt one thing at least. They brought back to England the habit of smoking tobacco.

Ralegh did not give up his schemes. He showed that he was ready to learn by what had gone wrong. Hariot told him that both tobacco and potatoes would be crops well worth growing. In talking to him, Ralegh realized that a successful community would have to do its own farming. He also decided that it ought to be a balanced community. This meant not only young men, but women and children as well.

So once again, in May, 1587, an expedition left Plymouth bound for Virginia. There were over a hundred settlers on board, including women and children. The leader was John White, the map-maker and artist of the previous expedition. They sailed to Roanoke Island, and went to look for the fifteen men whom Grenville had left behind. All that they found were houses, "overgrown with melons of divers sorts, and deer within them, feeding on those melons." No one has ever discovered what became of the fifteen men.

Meanwhile, the newcomers decided to stay at Roanoke. It was White's first failure to impose his will as a leader. The original plan was to go north to Chesapeake Bay. This had been discovered on the previous expedition, and was much more sheltered than Roanoke with better anchorage in rough weather. It was there that Jamestown was to be founded. The settlers ignored these advantages and stayed at Roanoke. On August 18th, 1587, a child called Virginia Dare was born. Her mother was John White's daughter, and she was the first child of English origin ever born in North America.

Virginia was christened, but rejoicings soon turned to worry. They were running short of supplies. Someone would have to go back to England to ask for more. There was a great deal of argument about who should go. In the end, White decided to abandon his charges and go himself.

He got home at a bad moment. Everyone's thoughts and energies were directed towards the coming conflict with Spain. The only boats White could find were two little pinnaces. They set out across the Atlantic, but were so harried by pirates that they had to turn home again. Then Grenville prepared three bigger ships for him. Before they could leave Bideford, they were forbidden to sail for America. Every ship that England could muster had to make straight for Plymouth to lie in wait for the Armada.

It was not until 1590 that White landed in Roanoke once again. As he approached, he saw smoke rising from where the settlement had been. No one came out to meet him, and the place was completely silent. He wandered around the deserted village, and found the letters CRO carved on a tree. Then he saw the word CROATOAN on a post of the stockade. Several chests had been buried, and then dug up again as if they had been looted.

White's party discussed what could have happened. Where had the settlers gone to, and had they left in a great hurry? White explained that *Croatoan* was the name of another island off the coast. The natives there were relations of the friendly Manteo. He had arranged before leaving that, if the settlers had to evacuate, they would carve the name of their destination. A cross over the word would show that there was trouble. Because there was no cross, the rescue party decided that all must be well. They never went any further to look for the settlers. Later they heard stories that some of them had been killed by Indians. They never heard what had happened to all the rest. Nobody knows to this day what became of little Virginia Dare.

The English had not yet succeeded in founding a colony. Ralegh did not despair. England, as well as Spain and France, was now in the race to settle America. He wrote, "I shall yet live to see it an English nation."

The troubles and glories of Richard Grenville and Walter Ralegh did not end in Virginia. In 1591, Grenville sailed out of Plymouth, this time not to colonise but on another instalment of war with Spain. The English were hoping to blockade Spain, and to seize the treasure fleet before it reached home. This would cripple Spain financially during the year to come.

Grenville anchored near the little town of Flores in the Azores. As so often happened, many of the seamen were ill. They were put ashore to recover. Grenville spent the time in taking on new ballast for his ships. Then suddenly, the news came that the Spanish fleet had appeared. Grenville and his six ships put to sea. They were in such a hurry that they did not even have time to let out all their sails.

They met the Spanish fleet and exchanged fire. The captains of the English ships realized that they were at a hopeless disadvantage. They were undermanned, and their ships, without proper ballast, were unsteady to handle. Under the cover of darkness, five of the ships slipped away. Only Grenville, in the little *Revenge*, was left.

The *Revenge* was one of the ships that were part of Hawkins' new deal for the English Navy. Drake had chosen her out of all the fleet to fight the Armada in. Like all Hawkins' ships, she was nimble, but this time she was not nimble enough. Grenville had been in no hurry to run away, and before he could do so, the Spanish fleet began to surround him. Their massive ships, twice the size of his own, towered over him and took all the wind out of his sails. He was trapped, and could only move "with the billows and the waves of the sea".

Grenville could have surrendered, but instead he began to fight. It was as if all his earlier life had been leading up to this moment. He was a man of almost demon-like energy, who had never been able to give his energy full expression. All the Virginian ventures with which he had been associated had failed. He had not been allowed to sail into the Pacific: Drake had gone there instead. Even at home, he had been overshadowed by Drake. But now he sensed a moment of glory which could be all his own.

One by one, the huge Spanish ships moved towards the little *Revenge*. They fired at her, and tried to grapple and board her. One by one, she repulsed them all. Her own condition became desperate, "filled with blood and the bodies of dead and wounded men . . . her masts all beaten overboard, all her tackle cut asunder, her upper works altogether razed." She was just the bare hulk of a ship slowly sinking into the water. She had almost no powder left.

But there was enough left to sink her. Grenville, mortally wounded, begged the master gunner to blow up the ship rather than surrender. The gunner agreed, but others on board made a pact with the Spaniards that they should be taken off the *Revenge* and ransomed home to England. This was done, and Grenville was carried on to the Spanish flag-ship. He was treated with courtesy and respect until he died of his wounds. As with so many other great sailors of his day, we do not know where he was buried. We do know that a mighty storm sprang up, and sank much of the Spanish fleet. The crippled *Revenge* herself went down. So the ship of Grenville, and

Drake, and Hawkins would never be towed in triumph into the ports of Spain.

Grenville's last fight was described by Sir Walter Ralegh, and was retold by Tennyson. Like Drake, Grenville has passed into the realms of legend. It was inevitable that he should be defeated, but to fight to the end against such impossible odds was a victory for the human spirit.

After Grenville's death, Ralegh's interest in Virginia came to an end. He turned his thoughts to a country then called Guiana in South America. Much of this country is now Venezuala.

He dreamed of finding gold. He knew that earlier in the century Spain had found fabulous riches in Mexico and Peru. Surely there might be another such country. A likely place was the mysterious jungles around the Orinoco and Amazon basins. Ralegh heard tales of a king, called El Dorado, or Golden Man. He was said to bathe in turpentine to make him sticky, and then roll in gold dust until it covered his whole body. The stories grew. There were tales of a great city, also called El Dorado. Ralegh sent one of his captains, Jacob Whiddon of Plymouth, to investigate. He came back with reports which filled Ralegh with hope.

So in February, 1595, Ralegh left Plymouth to sail for the mouths of the Orinoco. His journey to South America is described in his book, "The Discovery of the Large, Rich, and Beautiful Empire of Guiana." This book, more than any other, expresses the sheer joy of discovery, and the excitement which the Elizabethans felt in visiting new parts of the world. In Ralegh, the poet and man of action are blended together. Ralegh wrote about gentle hills and of winding rivers, of grass plains that were firm to ride on. The country abounded in wild life, and at evening the birds sang with a thousand different tunes, while the sun gleamed on their brilliant plumage: crimson, carnation, and white. Even while he exulted in all this beauty, he was thinking about the riches there were to be found. "Every stone that we stooped to take up promised either gold or silver by his complexion." He rejoiced that no one had been there before him. The country was "never sacked, turned, nor wrought, the face of the earth hath not been torn, nor the virtue and salt of the soil spent by manurance, the graves not opened for gold, the mines not broken with sledges, nor their images pulled down out of their temples."

Ralegh came home with fantastic stories. The playwright William Shakespeare listened to him, and made his hero Othello tell the same stories to Desdemona. Some people did not believe him. Ralegh thought they were narrow-minded. "There are stranger things to be seen in the world than are between London and Staines," he said contemptuously. In any case, he did not care what the general public thought. All he bothered about was the Queen. He had been out of her favour since marrying one of her waiting women. Elizabeth wanted her courtiers only to care for herself. Now he hoped to win back her interest with schemes for an empire in Guiana. He hoped in vain.

Ralegh's later life was tragic, on the heroic scale of those days. After Elizabeth's death, the new Stuart king, James I, accused him of treason, and imprisoned him for many years in the Tower of London. At last, he was released, and given permission to go again to Guiana to look for gold. James, like most other monarchs, wanted more ready money. He had come to believe Ralegh's theories that there might be gold in Guiana. He was not deterred by unpromising reports from Sir Thomas Roe, who had led an expedition from Plymouth that sailed far up the Amazon. So, in June 1617, Ralegh sailed once more from Plymouth. His whole future depended on what he could find. His ship, all too aptly, was called the *Destiny*.

Destiny was against him. He found no miraculous gold mines. Instead, he found that the Spanish had occupied the country since his former visit. His elder son, Wat, was killed. Angry reports were sent back to Spain of how Ralegh was interfering with Spanish rights. King James was anxious to be on good terms with Spain. He would only forgive Ralegh for gold, and there was no gold. When Ralegh returned, the King brought the old charges of treason against him. It seems a shabby, trumped-up affair, but Ralegh was sentenced to death.

When the Attorney-General called for the sentence, he made a strange statement. It shows how this great Elizabethan glimmered in the commonplace court of the Stuarts. "He hath been as a star at which the world gazed; but stars may fall, nay they must fall when they trouble the sphere wherein they abide."

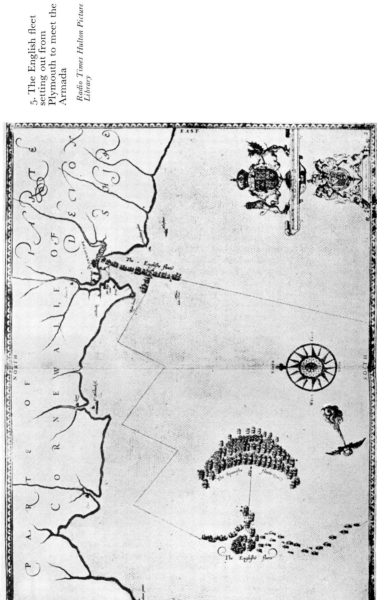

5. The English fleet setting out from Plymouth to meet the Armada

Radio Times Hulton Picture Library

6. Engagement between the English fleet and the Armada

12

The Day of the Companies

THE great seamen died, and the port of Plymouth went on. It had become a magnet for anybody who wanted to travel towards the west. New streets of houses were built, with alleys and courtyards winding away behind them. The town was still clustered tightly around the harbour. It was crowded, noisy, and smelly. A fort was built on the tongue of land between the Hoe and the harbour. Since the Armada, everybody had realized how vulnerable Plymouth would be if attacked by sea.

The town lived for the sea. Not only did it supply sailors, but more and more of its people came to earn their living by repairing ships or providing food and other supplies. In such a tightly-knit community, everyone knew what was happening. There was always news of fresh ventures.

Cavendish followed Drake through the Straits of Magellan and round the world. He set out once again in 1591, but he died on the journey. John Davis of Dartmouth, with whom he sailed, discovered the Falkland Islands. Davis was not a spectacular figure to appeal to the Plymouth crowds, but the seamen in the waterfront inns had plenty to say about him. He was a magnificent navigator. A few bold men maintained that he was far better than Drake. What no one with any knowledge denied was that his invention, the quadrant, was a great

4

help in navigating. It was used until the sextant was invented, more than a hundred years later.

Since this was Plymouth, there was plenty of talk about Richard Hawkins, Sir John's son and old William's grandson. He had inherited from his father a great concern for the conditions of men on board ship. To this he had added an almost fanatical belief in the value of fruit. He attributed magical powers to lemons and oranges, and said that if seamen would eat these fruits all the time the appalling disease of scurvy could be wiped out. The know-alls in the Plymouth inns laughed at him. One or two whispered that he did not have the same control over his men that his father or Drake had. Even so, there was mourning in Plymouth when Richard Hawkins sailed through the Straits of Magellan and then disappeared. News came that he was a prisoner of the Spaniards in Peru. He did not come home for many years, until after his father's death. When he got home, he wrote a book called *Observations* which is the best account of conditions at sea in his time. It was a tragedy for the Navy that his ideas about scurvy-preventing foods were not widely followed.

The Atlantic and America had made Plymouth famous, but still the English longed to trade with the Far East. They thought of it as the treasure house of the world, filled with spices, jewels, and shining exotic fabrics. The problem was how to get there. It was nearly a hundred years since the first Portuguese had sailed eastwards round the Cape of Good Hope, but no English captain had yet attempted the journey. They believed it to be very dangerous. They also believed, quite wrongly, that it would be a longer route than sailing through the Straits of Magellan and across the Pacific. There were no accurate means of measuring distance, and nobody had yet realized just how wide the Pacific was.

Then in 1591, an expedition with three ships left Plymouth to make the first English attempt to sail round the Cape of Good Hope. From the very start, things went badly. The sailors were soon attacked by their dreaded enemy, scurvy. It was made worse by torrential rain, which drenched the men. In the cramped, stuffy quarters below decks, they could not dry their clothes off. "We could not keep our men dry three hours together." As soon as they had rounded the Cape, they landed to get fresh supplies of food. So many men were ill by that time, that they sent one shipload of invalids home. Then a few days later, the *Penelope*, chief ship of the expedition, was lost in a terrible storm. Only the *Edward Bonaventure* under James Lancaster, was left. Four days after that, her men wondered if they too would be lost. The ship was struck by lightning. Four men were killed outright, and the others severely bruised to the point of bleeding. The main mast was shattered. "Some of the spikes that were ten inches deep into the timber were melted with the extreme heat thereof."

Despite everything, they managed to make their way across the Indian Ocean. They sailed to the islands of the East Indies; Sumatra, Java and Borneo. Here they preyed on Portuguese shipping, and captured cargoes like pepper. They heard tales of a consignment of fine cloths from India, and even a cargo of rubies and diamonds. By now, they no longer cared. Lancaster was very ill, and the men were determined to sail back to England without further delay.

Their journey back was another long-drawn-out agony. It brings home once again at what cost in human life and suffering these early voyages of exploration were made. They had to hang about for five weeks for a favourable wind to get round the Cape of Good Hope. Then they stopped off at St Helena where some of the men recovered their health by eating oranges and lemons; a proof that Richard Hawkins was right. Lancaster now wanted to sail across to Brazil to catch favourable winds home. The men nearly mutinied, and insisted on staying close to the African coast. They imagined that this would shorten their journey. Instead, they spent six weeks in the Doldrums, and finally had to run across to the West Indies in search of a wind. From there they tried to sail north. This time, there was too much wind, and they ran into storms. As so often, food became short. Lancaster went ashore with a party to look for food. Their ship either drifted away or deliberately deserted. There were then six men on the ship and nineteen on shore, compared to the ninety-seven alive when they first rounded the Cape.

Luckily, Lancaster reached home alive. A French ship finally brought him back, over three years after he left Plymouth. The Portuguese reckoned to do the same journey in eighteen months. On the face of it, he had not been very successful. In fact, his voyage proved extremely important.

Lancaster showed it was possible for the English to sail round Africa to the Far East. For two and a half centuries, this became the main English sea route to India and beyond. When the Suez Canal was shut in 1967, it became so again.

The voyage also stimulated English interest in trade with the Far East. In 1600, the East India Company was founded. Lancaster himself headed its first expedition. Nobody could yet know that the work of the company would lead to a long period of British rule in India. Once again, a voyage from Plymouth had helped to alter the whole course of history. It is therefore appropriate that the first Englishman ever sent as an ambassador to an Indian court should bear a famous Plymouth name: William Hawkins the third.

This success in breaking into the Far Eastern market reawakened interest in America. If there could be an East India Company, why not have a Virginia Company too? It might well succeed where individual efforts had failed. So the Virginia Company was founded, based on London and Plymouth. The man in charge of the Plymouth end of affairs was Sir Ferdinando Gorges. He was Governor of the newly-built Plymouth Fort, which stands on the site where the Citadel now is.

Gorges was a Somerset man himself, but was related to the Raleghs and Gilberts. Both his son and his brother had sailed to America on journeys sponsored by Ralegh. But what really fired his imagination was being given three Indians brought back from America by a captain called Waymouth. He had them taught to speak English, and then questioned them closely and with ever-growing interest. He afterwards said, "This accident must be acknowledged the means under God of putting on foot and giving life to all our plantations.''

In 1607, the Virginia Company sent two ships out of Plymouth. They were the *Gift of God*, and the *Mary and John* commanded by Ralegh Gilbert, son of Sir Humphrey. The way the same family names keep on cropping up show how closely these West Country families were linked in their enterprises.

Knowledge of the Atlantic was increasing fast. Sailors were now taking a direct route across it, which meant that they could explore the neglected part of the coast between Virginia and Newfoundland. In this case, they sailed to what is now Maine, to Sagadahoc on the Kennebec river. The ships returned in November, bringing good reports, but none of the cargo for which the company hoped. All was not well, however, with the small colony left behind. The men, as so often in early ventures, were those who had made a failure of life at home. The leaders had little control over them. It was an agonizingly cold winter. When a ship arrived in 1608, bringing supplies, everyone chose to go home. So ended the first English settlement in the northern United States.

For a little while, Plymouth faded out of the picture. The London Virginia Company founded a settlement called Jamestown at Chesapeake Bay. As earlier settlers had suspected, this was a promising place. At long last the English had a successful American colony. But London took all the credit.

Gorges did not lose interest in America. He met some more Indians who had been brought back to England. They inspired him to think that the English might, after all, adapt themselves to North American winters. He began to focus his interest on the area round Cape Cod, that is well north of Virginia, but south of the ill-fated Sagadahoc settlement. Then Captain John Smith appeared on the scene.

Of all the remarkable people concerned with the early links between England and America, Smith was one of the most extraordinary. As a young man, seeking adventure, he had gone out to fight the Turks. He had been left for dead on the battle field, found by the Turks, and sold into slavery. He escaped by killing his master. He made his way home to England, but, finding things there too quiet, went out to Virginia. His vigour and enterprise proved of the greatest value to the London Virginia Company. It was at this time that the best-known event in his life occurred. He was captured by Indians, and his life was saved by the young princess, Pocahontas. Later she married an Englishman called John Rolfe and came back to Plymouth with him.

Smith did not stay in Virginia long. He was another of these men of such fantastic energy that more commonplace people found it hard to get on with him. In 1614, he set off northwards to explore the American seaboard. He was the first Englishman to make any detailed survey of the area north of Virginia. As he travelled, he gave English names to the Indian villages that he found. Of one village he wrote, "Then you come to Accomack, an excellent good harbour, good land, and no want of anything but industrious people." By what was to prove an extraordinary coincidence, he gave the place the name Plymouth.

When Smith returned to England, he sought out Gorges. He hoped they might work together in rivalry to the London Virginia Company. Their conversations probably led to the use of the name "New England" to describe the country Smith had explored. Smith's *Description of New England* was published in 1616, and it has been known by that name ever since. Otherwise, there was little to show for what had seemed a promising partnership. Three attempts to leave Plymouth with expeditions all failed, and Smith and Gorges discovered that they did not work well together.

However, Smith had increased Gorges' interest in New England. This became even more fervent when an Indian called Squanto was brought to Plymouth. Squanto, though no one yet knew it, was to play an important part in American history. One of Gorges' captains, sent to explore, brought further encouraging reports. Gorges applied for a patent to colonize New England. The Plymouth Virginia Company was now in direct rivalry with the London branch.

At last, Gorges came to play his part in history. News of his activities reached the ears of some English exiles at Leyden in Holland. They were thinking of emigrating to America. They now decided to go to New England rather than to Virginia. When the Pilgrim Fathers landed in America, it was at the place already called Plymouth, and marked with that name on John Smith's map. When they wanted official permission to occupy the land there, it was to Gorges that they applied.

There is a fine and elaborate monument to the Gorges family in St Budeaux church in Plymouth. It was restored by the citizens of Maine, U.S.A. in memory of

Sir Ferdinando Gorges. In their inscription they call him "First Proprietor and Governor" of Maine.

The work of the Virginia Company has another, more famous memorial.

In 1609, a fleet left Plymouth to reinforce the English colony in Virginia. The *Sea Venture*, commanded by Sir George Somers, was wrecked in a frightening storm. The survivors described what happened.

> "At length did beat all light from heaven; which like an hell of darkness did turn black upon us . . . only upon the Thursday night, Sir George Somers being upon the watch, had an apparition of a little round light, like a faint star, trembling and streaming along with a sparkling blaze, half the height upon the main mast, and shooting sometimes from shroud to shroud . . . half the night it kept with us; running sometimes along the mainyard to the very end, and then returning."

They were cast up on the islands of Bermuda. This was a dreaded spot, believed to have "such tempests, thunders, and other fearful objects . . . no habitation of men, but rather given over to Devils and Wicked Spirits." In fact, they passed an agreeable winter there. Next spring, they sailed for Virginia in two pinnaces built out of the wood of the wrecked *Sea Venture*.

News of the shipwreck reached England. Accounts of it were circulated among members of the Virginia Company and their friends. One of these friends was fascinated by the idea of the great storm at sea and the island haunted by spirits. He thought that one of those spirits might have appeared as the light on the rigging. He remembered other accounts he had read, of the strange habits and dances of the American Indians. He thought of the joy that explorers had found in strange countries,

and the lure of smooth, yellow sands. William Shakespeare
started to write *The Tempest*.

In one way, *The Tempest* is magical poetry. In another
way, it is frightening and prophetic. Shakespeare wrote of
the first inhabitant of the island, Caliban, which may
just mean a cannibal of the Caribbean. At first he welcomed the settlers, and then he came to resent them.

> "When thou camst first,
> Thou strok'st me, and made much of me; would'st
>   give me
> Water with berries in't; and teach me how
> To name the bigger light, and how the less,
> That burn by day and night: and then I loved thee,
> And showed thee all the qualities o' th'isle,
> The fresh springs, brine-pits, barren place and fertile:
> Curs'd be that I did so . . .
> For I am all the subjects that you have,
> Which first was mine own King: and here you sty me
> In this hard rock, whiles you do keep from me
> The rest of th'island."

The newcomers reproach Caliban for being ungrateful.

> "I pitied thee,
> Took pains to make thee speak, taught thee each
>   hour
> One thing or other: when thou didst not, savage,
> Know thine own meaning, but would gabble like
> A thing most brutish, I endow'd thy purposes
> With words that made them known."

Caliban's answer is simple.

> "You taught me language; and my profit on't
> Is, I know how to curse."

Other men were still merely talking about founding
colonies. Shakespeare saw the tragic dilemma that it
would involve.

13

"A Special Providence"

SO FAR, it had been the rich and the famous who tried to found settlements in America. Now came the turn of some very ordinary people. There was a weaver, a cloth-maker, a tailor, and a carpenter. There was a man who made barrels, and also a smith. With them went their wives and children. As individuals they might have seemed quite unimportant. As a group, they were the most famous ship-load that ever sailed out of Plymouth. They are known as the Pilgrim Fathers.

Their reasons for going to America were different from those of all earlier settlers. They did not care about either adventure or money. They wanted freedom to worship God in their own way.

In their time, there was only one lawful church in England. Henry VIII had broken away from the Church of Rome. He had made the King or Queen of England supreme head of the church in place of the Pope. But the Church of England kept several important features of the Roman Catholic Church. It had a system of church government based on bishops. It kept a set form of services, although the language used was English, not Latin. The changes were attacked by those who thought they had gone too far, and also by those who thought they had not gone far enough.

The second group were called "Puritans", because they believed they could purify religion, and bring it back to the simple days of the Apostles. A band of such people met at Scrooby in Nottinghamshire, to hold their own type of service. Their pastor; they naturally shunned the word "priest"; was a man called John Robinson. By the standards of the time, he was quite moderate in his opinions. Even so, the Scrooby congregation was persecuted. Disloyalty to the church was seen as disloyalty to the head of the church, James I. Some of the Scrooby men were imprisoned. Others had the nerve-racking experience of knowing that they were being watched day and night. They decided that life in England was impossible for them. They wanted to go somewhere where they could worship in freedom. The Netherlands, which was staunchly Protestant, seemed the best place.

It was one thing to decide to go, and another to get there. They had to bribe a ship's captain before he would take them on board. Then he betrayed them to the authorities. They were stopped, and thoroughly searched. All were stripped of their money and other belongings. Some were put into prison.

This only made them more determined. Next spring, 1608, they tried again. This time the men of the congregation managed to get away. They met terrible storms out at sea. They tossed and groaned, but meanwhile the women and children were in an even worse state. The men had been in such a hurry to get away that they had left their families in a small boat stuck in the mud. Fortunately, the English authorities decided that they were more nuisance than they were worth. They packed them all off to join their husbands and fathers in Holland.

So, from the first, the Scrooby congregation were people who met hardship. From the first, hardship brought out tremendous reserves of patience and endurance in them. They never cursed God when things went wrong, but gave thanks whenever they were saved from worse troubles. One of the congregation, William Bradford, wrote a detailed account of their lives. It was not known until it was found at Fulham Palace in London in 1856. Again and again, Bradford uses the phrase, "a special providence". This shows how they believed that God was caring for them among all their difficulties.

Life in Holland did not prove easy for them. They thought that the customs of the country were strange, and they found it hard to get their tongues round the language. Most of them were farming people, but they had to learn new trades in order to earn a living. Even so, they had a constant struggle with poverty. They began to worry about their children. Would they accept such a hard, stern way of life? Or would the distractions of Leyden, the university city where they had settled, prove too tempting for them? There was also the risk that Holland might once again be attacked by Catholic Spain. They had not fled from the Church of England to risk being ruled by Roman Catholics. Once more they looked round for somewhere where they could pursue their own ideas in peace. This time, they thought of America.

The obvious place was Virginia, but they were worried that there, too, they might be persecuted for their religious ideas. They petitioned the Virginia Company for permission to form a colony, and asked if their freedom of worship could be guaranteed. The best they could get was a promise that they would not be molested. They argued about whether to settle for this. Soon, their arguments became bitter. Like almost everyone else in the seventeenth century, the Pilgrims were fiercely intolerant of anyone who disagreed with themselves.

It was at this point that they first heard of Gorges' plans to develop New England. They knew that the area at least had good fishing, as one of the earliest place names, Cape Cod, shows. They decided that this was where they should go.

More difficulties still beset them. They had no money to buy a ship and to set out on their own. They would have to find someone to back them. In the end, some London merchants agreed, but they struck a very hard bargain. They would pay for the ships and supplies for the colonists, but the colonists in return would have to work seven years for a bare living. During this time, all profits would be taken by the promoters. The Pilgrims asked to have two days a week to work for themselves. Even this was denied them.

Because of these harsh conditions, many people decided they would not go. The Leyden congregation now numbered nearly three hundred. Not much over a tenth were willing to risk life in America, and that included women and children who had no choice in the matter. Very few of this small group came from the original Scrooby congregation. Their pastor, John Robinson, decided that his duty lay to stay with the majority. Two of the Scrooby men who decided to go had the sort of qualities which would prove of great value in a new community. They were "Elder" Brewster and William Bradford.

Bradford's attitude to the venture is summed up in the way he described their departure from Leyden. "So they left the goodly and pleasant city which had been their resting place near twelve years, but they knew they were pilgrims, and looked not so much on those things but lift up their eyes to the heavens, their dearest country, and quieted their spirits."

At Southampton they met the rest of the party whom the promoters of the expedition had found to go with them. The Leyden group found themselves outnumbered. In order to keep their own sense of identity, they referred to the others as "Strangers". To themselves they gave the name "Saints", using the word in the Biblical sense of "God's chosen people".

The Saints began to take stock of their new companions. They found that most of them came from London, especially from a district around Aldgate. Many of them, like the Saints themselves, had a country background a generation or so back. They had the same sorts of jobs as the Saints, small tradesmen, craftsmen, or working men. A few of them employed servants, who were also coming, but that was no proof of any great wealth in those days. No one among the newcomers was any more famous than they were themselves. They were told that Captain John Smith had offered to come, to teach the colonists how to defend themselves in case of attack. He had asked a ridiculous fee. Somebody brandished a copy of Smith's book on New England, and said it was very much better value than Smith himself.

Then the Saints met the man who was coming instead of Smith to train them in fighting. His name was Miles Standish. The Saints decided that he was the sort of man they could get on with, and that he would prove a valuable person to have. They were much more dubious about one or two of the Strangers. In particular there was a family called the Billingtons, who used quite deplorable language. Later, when somebody nearly blew their ship up by throwing squibs in the powder kegs, everyone knew that it was the Billington boy.

Nearly half the party were women and children. The women wondered what lay ahead, and in what sort of conditions their next children would be born. The children eyed one another curiously, then began to exchange names. Some had common names like John, Mary, and Elizabeth. One was called Damaris, out of the New Testament. But three of them had to admit that their names were Love, Wrestling, and Resolved.

There were still more delays and problems in raising

money. At long last, they left Southampton. They had two ships: the *Speedwell*, which had brought the Saints over from Holland, and the larger *Mayflower*. Before they had got very far, it was obvious that the *Speedwell* was leaking badly. They put in to Dartmouth where she was thoroughly checked and repaired. Once again, they set out. They sailed on past Land's End, and told one another that this was their last sight of England. Then the *Speedwell* started to leak again. They were three hundred miles from the English coast when the captain decided that they would have to turn back. It seemed wisest for the two ships to keep together. So both headed for the nearest big port in the far south-west of England. The *Speedwell* and the *Mayflower* sailed in to Plymouth.

In Plymouth, they had further long discussions about what to do. They feared that the *Speedwell* would never be fit to make the Atlantic crossing. In fact, she later proved sound enough when she carried shorter masts and less sail. At the time, it seemed that their only choice was to abandon their plans, or to cram as many people as possible into the *Mayflower*. It was the moment for any doubters to drop out, and a number did. There were still too many to fit on to the *Mayflower*, so the families with large numbers of very young children agreed not to go.

The rest of the party settled down to their last night in England. They stayed by Sutton Pool to be near the *Mayflower*. Two places are still pointed to as the spot where they stayed: a house with high, pointed gables called Island House, and the cellars of a wine merchant's warehouse. Then they went along a quay jutting out into the harbour to embark on their journey. A few on-lookers watched them, but their going aroused no particular interest in a port that had seen so many more famous people.

As they cast off, the Pilgrims stared round for their last look at Plymouth. Between Sutton Pool and the

Sound was Plymouth Fort. It was interesting to them because of Sir Ferdinando Gorges. Nearer to them, overlooking the quay, was the old castle of Plymouth, with its four towers. Only a trace of one tower now remains, but the four, along with St Andrew's cross, are still shown on the city's coat of arms. The city's motto might well have been taken by the Pilgrims themselves: *The strongest tower is the name of the Lord.*

So the *Mayflower* sailed. The passengers explored what was to be their home. They found that she was about ninety foot bow to stern, twenty-five foot in extreme breadth, and some seventeen foot deep. Her capacity was a hundred and eighty tons, which meant, by the system still used, that she could carry a hundred and eighty very large casks of wine. Instead, she was crammed with a hundred passengers, and all their worldly belongings, as well as her own crew. There was very little room to spare. Quarters below decks were very cramped, and only the smaller women and the children could stand fully upright. Luckily, she was said to be a "sweet" ship. That meant that she had been engaged in the Mediterranean wine-trade, and smelt of wine and not something like salt cod. It was not long before she ceased to be sweet, with so many people packed tightly together, no water for washing, and no sanitation at all.

The passengers were condemned to the common diet of seafarers at that time. This was salt meat, dry fish, hard biscuits, cheese and beer. They learnt that they were fortunate if the food was not actually mouldy. Soon, they ran into gales. At times, the winds were so fierce that they had to haul down all sails, and abandon themselves to the battering of the waves for days on end. They tossed to and fro at random. The ship strained and creaked, and pulled apart at the seams. They rushed round, caulking the leaks. There was a crisis when a main beam bent and cracked. Mercifully, they could fasten it up with a large

iron screw brought from Holland, another example of
God's special mercy to them. Then there was another
crisis when one of their servants, John Howland, was
flung overboard. He caught hold of a trailing rope,
which played out to its full length. He hung on, but still
he sank deeper and deeper. The others hauled desperately
at the rope. As he came up to the surface, they grabbed at
him with a boat-hook. He was still alive.

They had been over two months at sea by the time
they sighted Cape Cod. The direct route had taken them
longer than many ships took going by the West Indies.
In spite of everything, only one passenger died; a good
record for those days. A boy was born, among all the
storms, and in cramped and crowded quarters. He was
given the name Oceanus.

Already they had been through enough to make anybody despair. Instead of this, their endurance was
deepened, as was their willingness to praise God for any
mercies. This was indeed a different breed of settlers
from those who had gone before. "It is not with us as
with other men whom small things can discourage," said
Brewster. Bradford, who was the first man to call them
"Pilgrims", foretold what future generations would say.
"Our fathers were Englishmen which came over this
great ocean, and were ready to perish in this wilderness;
but they cried unto the Lord, and he heard their voice."

14

"One Small Candle"

A NOVEMBER sea, grey and cold, stretched end-
lessly behind, cutting the newcomers off from all
contact with home and friends. The sky was over-
cast, and rain was falling, mingled with flurries of snow.
Ahead were barren sand dunes. The land in the distance was covered with deep, secretive-looking woods, in
which enemies might lurk. Everything was withering,
and soon the earth would be locked with frost. This was
the New World as the Pilgrims first saw it.

They had come further north than they intended, and
wanted to sail south. The weather, and a dread of reefs,
were against them. They stayed in the bay formed by
Cape Cod, which points up northwards like an encircl-
ing arm. A party of men went ashore to try to find somewhere to settle. They had to use small boats, for the
sailors refused to bring the *Mayflower* to shore until they
were certain of good anchorage. Soon after they landed,
they saw "savages", to whom they did not speak. They
heard a hideous cry, which they thought must be wolves.
The whole country seemed very hostile. When night
came, they built a fire, and round it a rough barricade.
They huddled inside.

Then came their first bit of luck. They found a place
where corn had been planted and cut. Nearby were the
remains of a house. There was no sign of anyone living
there, but there were newly-made mounds of sand, on

which the marks of hands were still visible. Was it a
roughly-made grave? They disturbed the sand, not knowing what to expect, and found baskets full of ears of corn.
They had seed for their next year's harvest.

A month passed. They resigned themselves to winter-
ing round Cape Cod. The pilot now offered to bring the
Mayflower to land. He said he had been in the country
before, and knew how to find a safe harbour. He mistook
the place, and they were caught in a storm of rain and
snow. They passed a night wretched with wet and cold.
Some of them struggled on to an island to light fires to
warm themselves. Next morning, the Sabbath, the sun
was shining. On Monday, they went ashore. At last, they
had found a place where they might settle. There was
anchorage for the *Mayflower*, and there were streams of
running water. The place seemed to be fertile, for there
were fields there. Once it had been an Indian settlement,
but it was now deserted. That meant that they might
expect to be left in peace. It was much the best place they
had seen, and they decided to stay there. One of the
first men to visit the colony wrote, "After the planters had
failed of their intention, and the pilot of his, it pleased
Almighty God (who had better provided for them than
their own hearts could imagine) to plant them upon the
seat of an old town which divers years before had been
abandoned of the Indians." The town was the one called
Accomack, or, as John Smith had renamed it, Plymouth.

Their first need was to build a shelter for common use.
They had only such tools as they had brought with them,
and no means of forging metal for any more. So the
building had to be simple. They looked at the remains of
the Indian houses, and decided to copy them. As John
White's drawings had already shown, the east coast
Indians did not live in conical tents, but in oblong huts
with rounded roofs. They were made of a timber frame-
work, hung over with bark or skins. The Pilgrims built

such a house for themselves. Glass for the windows was a luxury that they could not even hope for. They had no means of making glass. They did have the thin skins of animal bladders to serve instead. Later on in the seventeenth century, settlers from northern Europe started to build the log cabins with which they were familiar at home. These provided much better shelter than the Indian-style house that the Pilgrims had.

The bleak New England winter set in. It was another time of great trial for the Pilgrims. While they were riding at anchor, Bradford's young wife, Dorothy, had fallen from the ship and been drowned. A few days before, Susannah White had borne a child on the *Mayflower*. He was called Peregrine, from the Latin word for one who travels in a strange country. The Pilgrims started to try to establish themselves on shore. Disease struck them. The "common house" was turned into a hospital. Sometimes there were only six or seven people on their feet. They had to fetch wood, make fires, prepare food, and look after the sick. It was almost impossible to keep warm. Then, to make things worse still, the common house caught fire in the middle of January. The Pilgrims, used to damp English winters, had not allowed for the drier American air. They had to find somewhere quickly to put the sick people. Fortunately, the *Mayflower* was riding out the winter off-shore and waiting for better weather to sail home. They ferried boat-loads of invalids out to her. Most of the sailors were ill as well. They commented on the way that the Pilgrims nursed one another willingly and cheerfully, compared to their own bad humour. But devotion was not enough. By the end of the winter, no less than half the Pilgrims were dead.

Earlier colonists had given up after suffering very much less. The Pilgrims might well have despaired. Instead, these astonishing people thought it was thanks to God's "special providence" that as many as half of their number were still alive. It is their faith that sets them apart from previous colonists. Their faith helped them to endure all their sufferings, and, at moments, to rise in triumph above them. It has made the Pilgrims a symbol of all the courage, endurance, and hope that are needed to build a great nation.

All through that terrible winter, they were living from day to day. Nobody ever knew who would be alive to see next day's sunrise. It would have been very easy to forget all wider issues. Yet, from the first, the Pilgrims saw that they would have to organize their society in some way. All previous colonies had gone out with a ready-appointed governor. The Pilgrims had none. So before leaving the *Mayflower*, on November 11th, 1620, they drew up a formal compact. They combined themselves into "a civil Body Politic" with the right to enact laws. They promised "all due submissiveness and obedience to such laws." By common consent, they chose John Carver as Governor for the first year.

In this way, a self-governing community was established, right in the earliest days of American colonial history. The compact was not unique, for a House of Burgesses had already met in Virginia. This had been elected by the votes of all adult men, whereas with the *Mayflower* compact only four of the serving men signed. Nonetheless, the *Mayflower* compact was far ahead of the England of its own time. It showed the way that America would develop, and so has become a significant part of American history.

At long last, the winter was over. Spring brought new hopes. In March, to their great astonishment, an Indian came to the settlement who was able to speak English. This was the same Squanto who had been taken to Plymouth and given to the Governor of Plymouth Fort. An early account of the colony actually calls him "Sir Ferdinando Gorges his Indian." Once more, New and old Plymouth were linked together.

Squanto had returned to America not long before the Pilgrims. He had found that most of his own people had died of the plague. This was why the settlement had been deserted. He was delighted to find new companions, and proved invaluable. He showed them how they could catch fish in the brook. When the weather improved, he helped them to plant the ears of Indian corn, or maize, that they had found. Before they did so, he made them manure the land, as the Indians did, with fish. The Pilgrims also planted seed they had brought from England. As the summer went on, they saw that none of their own seeds came up, but the Indian corn all flourished. While they were waiting for it to ripen, Squanto showed them which wild plants they could eat.

Another setback came in April. One hot day, John Carver, their governor, was sowing seed in the fields. He was suddenly taken ill, and died a few days later. William Bradford was chosen to follow him. Then Mrs Carver died too. For a moment it looked as if the events of the winter might be repeated. All was well. Those who had survived to that point proved to be very strong, and most of them lived on for many more years. The ship-born baby, Peregrine White, lived into the eighteenth century. He is famous for the number of his descendants.

It very soon became obvious that they must depend on themselves, without help from England. When the *Mayflower* returned, they did not send back any cargo. The reason for this was their sickness during the winter, but they were severely reproached. Another small ship-load of men came out from England to join them, and was greeted eagerly. They proved more hindrance than help, for they were quite unprepared for the sort of life that they found. They brought no supplies or tools with them. To make things more difficult, the Indian tribes around began to be troublesome. Squanto managed to keep them at bay by saying the English had plague buried in the ground, and had magical powers to make it come out again.

To their great joy, their harvest of Indian corn succeeded. As autumn came, flocks of birds arrived, including wild turkeys. For a short and wonderful moment, they had a feeling of plenty. Some time during the autumn, nobody knows just when, they ate their first harvest thanksgiving. It was another of their contributions to American folk-lore.

Life never became easy for these pioneers. Their story was one of continuing hardship and struggle, of disappointments from England, and the same shining faith in God's mercy. They made their mistakes, and tried to learn from them. Early on, they had communal property, but they decided that it would be better to give each family its own plot of land. "This had very good success; for it made all hands very industrious," Bradford wrote. "The women now went willingly into the fields and took their little ones with them to set corn, which before would allege weakness and inability." He thought it was wrong to believe "that the taking away of property and bringing them in community into a commonwealth, would make them happy and flourishing." This belief in individual enterprise was to become a central feature of American life.

Already, in these early days, New England was acquiring a character of its own. It was quite different from Virginia. The Virginian settlers were land-owners with large farms. As the tobacco industry developed, many of them became rich. They behaved like aristocrats with many servants and, later, slaves. They kept links with important people in England, and with the established church. In contrast, New England grew up around small towns. The most important building in each town was a "meeting house". The word "church" was never used, because it offended Puritan beliefs. The rich

people, and some became very rich, still kept to the way
of life of middle-class town-dwellers.

When the Civil War broke out in England in 1640,
the New Englanders sympathized with the Puritan,
Parliament side. The Virginians would have been for the
Church and the King. Two hundred years later, the
northern and southern United States had their own
Civil War. Its origins go right back to the very earliest
settlers, who had such different interests from the start.

The Plymouth settlement was very nearly forgotten.
In 1630 there was a great emigration under the Massachusetts Bay Company. This led to the foundation of
Boston. Plymouth was overshadowed. In 1691, it was
incorporated into the Massachusetts Bay Colony. For the
rest of the time Britain ruled America, nobody thought of
Plymouth as very important. Then America became
independent. The second President of the United States,
John Quincy Adams, was impressed by the *Mayflower*
compact. He spoke about it as one of the foundation-
stones of American democracy. Then, in the mid-
nineteenth century, Bradford's account of the colony was
discovered by chance in London. Since then, the fame of
Plymouth has grown and spread. Bradford himself foretold this. He wrote, "as one small candle may light a
thousand, so the light here kindled hath shone to many,
yea in some sort to our whole nation".

PART III

AN UNKNOWN LAND IN THE SOUTH

"I who had ambition not only to go farther than anyone had been before, but as far as it was possible to go."

Captain James Cook

15

A New Challenge

ON THE quays around Sutton Harbour, people began to talk about the old days. Where was Drake, where were Ralegh, Grenville and Gilbert? Even the lesser figures, like Cavendish, and Oxenham, and John Davis, seemed greater than anyone now. Sir Richard Hawkins was dead. Had the family vigour run down at last? There was no sign that a fourth-generation Hawkins would make Plymouth still more famous.

Then, suddenly, Plymouth had something much worse to worry about than its vanished glory. It had to fight for its life. In 1640, Civil War broke out between King and Parliament. The nation began the hideous process of tearing itself apart. Plymouth supported the Parliament side. From 1643 until 1646, it was besieged. At the worst moments, the town was completely surrounded by Royalist guns, and its water supplies cut off. There was no escape even by sea, for the enemy guns commanded the Cattewater. Trade and industry came to a stand-still. Ships rotted away by the quays. Thousands of people died, some from the fighting, but more through lack of food. In their weakened state, many others were carried off by disease. At last the war came to an end, and Parliament won. The people of Plymouth were told that their stand had helped to change the whole course of the war in the south-west. They waited eagerly for Parliament to give them some help or reward. Nothing came.

All Parliament did for Plymouth was to add one other great name to the glorious list of seamen who had sailed from the port. Admiral Robert Blake was a Somerset man, who fought both the Dutch and the Spaniards. His last expedition, in 1656, aroused memories of Drake's exploits. He captured a fleet from Brazil bringing treasure home to Spain; blockaded the Spanish coast during the winter; and then went into Santa Cruz, a small, well-fortified harbour, where he destroyed sixteen ships. He died on his way home, in Plymouth Sound, within sight of the port. His heart was buried in St Andrew's, like that of Sir Martin Frobisher, Drake's old rival.

The monarchy was restored, and Charles II came to the throne. Would he bear Plymouth a grudge for having opposed his father? News came that Gorges' old Fort was to be replaced by a new Citadel, to make the town even more safe against foreign invaders. The people of Plymouth watched doubtfully as the Citadel was built. There was a long sweep of grey stone wall rising above the rocks of the Hoe. That would serve to defend the town, they agreed. But how about the landward wall, with its splendid, elaborate gateway? The people of Plymouth were quick to notice that there were guns all round the Citadel. Some were directed out to sea, but others pointed straight at the town itself. It was some time before Plymothians were convinced that those guns would never be used.

Something else very important for Plymouth happened in Charles' reign. A man called Samuel Pepys was appointed Secretary to the Navy. Plymouth sailors scoffed when they heard about it. What did Pepys know about ships? He never went out on the open sea until he sailed from Plymouth to Tangiers at the age of fifty. Even then, he could not have learnt very much. By all reports, he was too busy being sick. The scoffers were utterly wrong. Nobody since John Hawkins had shown such dedication to the cause of the English Navy. Pepys withstood vicious attacks from those who opposed his work. He saw his achievements undone by others, and had to start all over again.

Pepys triumphed, and the Navy increased in size. It gradually became clear that it would need a new dock-yard, to build and repair its ships. So far, all this work was done in the south and east, at Woolwich, Deptford, Chatham, and Portsmouth. The idea grew that it would be useful to have a dockyard down in the far south-west. Plymouth, with all its naval associations, seemed an obvious place.

It was necessary to choose a site. Plymouth was still a compact place centred around Sutton Harbour. The streets were narrow and crowded. There was another small village, Stonehouse, clustered around Stonehouse Creek. Both of these were rejected, as being too cramped. Instead, it was decided to build the new dockyard out on the banks of the Tamar estuary, the Hamoaze. There was a fine, wide stretch of water, with a deep water channel. Whoever chose the spot had an eye to the future. The Hamoaze can now take ships like the air-craft carriers, *Eagle* and *Ark Royal*, which are bigger by far than anything ever dreamed of in the days of wooden-built sailing ships.

Plymouth Dock, commonly known as "Dock", was begun in 1691. It was a lonely and desolate place, separated from Plymouth by fields and marshes. At first the workmen lived afloat in old hulks moored in the river. Then a town began to grow up, later to be known by the more dignified name of "Devonport". It was built of the same local grey stone as Plymouth, but it had an entirely different character. Plymouth still had narrow streets, and twisting alleys. Its buildings were often irregular in shape, as if they had grown bit by bit.

The new town was built in a regular, classical style, with wide streets and balanced façades. As time went on, it had massively blank stone walls, hiding naval establishments as big as a palace. For acres, there was nothing in sight but grey stone with water beyond. The place had a strange, austere, almost forbidding elegance, brought to life by the endless bustle of all that was happening.

For Plymouth Dock was a fast-growing place. A hundred years after the first ships went there, it was bigger than Plymouth itself. There was no longer any risk that Plymouth would slip back into being just another small fishing port. Even so, it began to seem as if the great days of exploration were over. But the world still offered a major challenge to the men who sailed out of Plymouth: the mystery of the Pacific.

The Pacific covers a much larger area than anything else in the world. This becomes clear if one looks at a globe with the Pacific towards one and the equator at eye-level. Almost everything that one can see is sea.

People living in small, compact Europe simply could not imagine such an expanse of water. For hundreds of years they assumed that there must be a continent hidden in the Pacific. In the sixteenth century, Mercator claimed that there must be a vast southern continent to balance all the countries up in the north. Otherwise, he argued, the earth would be lop-sided, and would topple out of its position in space. He put the continent on a map, with the name of *Terra Australis Incognita*, the unknown land in the south.

This was the Terra Australis that comes into the stories of Grenville and Drake. It was believed to be very rich, even richer than India and the Far East. The writings of Marco Polo, the mediaeval traveller, were quoted as proof of this. Nobody realized that he had been mistranslated.

Magellan sailed into the Pacific in 1522. Drake and

then Cavendish followed him fifty years later. After they went through the Straits of Magellan, the winds and currents carried them up northwards towards the Equator. Later sailors stayed on this same northward course, so that there were huge areas of the Pacific that no European had ever been to at all. The ocean guarded its secrets. Nobody even knew just how wide it was, for there was no accurate method of measuring longitude. It is, in fact, up to ten thousand miles east to west at its widest point, and a similar distance from north to south. Some early estimates of its width were three thousand miles too little; that is the distance between London and New York.

The first person who nearly solved the mysteries of the Pacific was a Dutchman called Tasman. He went further south than earlier sailors and found Van Diemen's Land, now Tasmania, and New Zealand. On a later voyage, he found the north coast of Australia. This was in the sixteen forties, when everybody in England was busy with civil war. Unfortunately for Tasman, his employers, the Dutch East India Company, were not at all impressed. They said that such poor, uncivilized countries could not possibly be the famous Terra Australis. This is a classic example of people looking for what they think ought to be there and not for what really is there. Such attitudes were another reason why the discovery of the Pacific was so slow.

Another hundred years passed. Then, in the mid-eighteenth century, there came a number of voyages that helped to arouse new interest in the Pacific. One of these was by a Frenchman called Bougainville. His name is now partly remembered for a plant called bougainvillea which he brought back from his journey. It covers walls all around the Mediterranean with splashes of vivid purple. The other three voyages were by British captains. All of them sailed from Plymouth.

The first to sail was "Foul Weather Jack", or, to give
him his proper name, Commodore the Hon. John Byron.
He, too, is remembered for something apart from his
voyage. His grandson became a poet. He sailed in 1764
with two ships, the *Dolphin* and *Tamar*. His sailing orders
arouse memories of the great Elizabethans. He was to
sail to the South Atlantic and take possession of the
Falkland Islands for Britain. The Falklands had been
discovered by John Davis on a voyage starting from
Plymouth. After that, Byron was to sail up the west coast
of the Americas to Drake's old harbour of Nova Albion.
Then, once again like Drake, he was to search for
the North-West Passage from the Pacific into the
Atlantic.

Byron followed the first part of his orders, and laid
claim to the Falkland Islands. He then sailed into the
Pacific, and took a course of his own. He wanted to try
to locate the Solomon Islands, which were known to
exist, although no one was sure where they were. Some
people believed that they were the off-shore islands of
the unknown southern continent.

Like others before him, he went a bit far to the north,
and so missed the Solomon Islands. He did discover a
number of other islands, never visited by Europeans
before. These included the group now called the Gilbert
Islands, to one of which he gave his own name. They
anchored off-shore to avoid the fiercely pounding surf,
and the Gilbertese came out in canoes to meet them.
Byron found them a friendly, handsome, cheerful, and
thieving people.

When Byron reached home, two years after leaving,
his account of his discoveries interested the Admiralty
very much. They decided to send another expedition to
explore the Pacific. Captain Samuel Wallis was chosen
as commander instead of Byron. Philip Carteret, who
had been first lieutenant on the *Dolphin*, was put in com-

7. Mayflower II. A replica of the Pilgrims' ship,
which sailed in 1957

Radio Times Hulton Picture Library

8. Captain James Cook, by Webber

National Portrait Gallery

mand of a second ship called the *Swallow*. They left
Plymouth in August 1766.

The *Dolphin* was used again. She was a sound ship, and
had been "copper-bottomed". That is, she was sheathed
with copper-plate to protect her against the wood-eating
worms that flourished in tropical waters. She was well
fitted-out and supplied for the expedition. Among other
things, she carried some "portable soup", little, hard
tablets of soup powder similar to modern stock cubes.
This was thought to be of use in preventing scurvy. Such
soup can still be seen at Greenwich today. In contrast,
the *Swallow* was very badly equipped, and made heavy
going across the Atlantic. They sailed into Magellan's
Straits. As earlier sailors had found, this was a wretched
place at the best of times, with intense cold, gusting
winds, and high, forbidding cliffs. It took them four
months to get through, which was one of the longest
passages on record, and one of the most unpleasant.
Worse was to come. The *Dolphin* sailed out of the Straits
into a thick, muffling blanket of fog. She could not see or
hear the *Swallow*. There were high waves and strong
winds, so it was impossible to turn back and look for her.
They never met again.

Wallis sailed on into the Pacific. He found a group of
islands, the Tuamotus, and then he came to Tahiti. Both
he and his first lieutenant were sick at the time. It was
his second lieutenant who went ashore to cut a sod of
earth and to take possession of the island in the name
of King George III. This man was Tobias Furneaux of
Swilly, then a small place near Plymouth, and now a
part of the city.

Tropical, south-sea islands have become a sort of
dreamland, the ideal of everyone who longs "to get away
from it all." Tahiti was the perfect tropical island. It was
spectacularly beautiful, with magnificent mountains rising to seven thousand feet only a few miles away from

5

the sea. With water all round it, there were magical effects of light and of atmosphere. The climate was hot, but not oppressive, and torrents of pure, fresh water streamed down from the mountains. Everywhere, there were lush, vividly-coloured plants. The people had lightish-brown skins and were well-proportioned. Some of the girls were exceptionally beautiful by any standards. They washed three times a day, which was more than Europeans did at the time, and their clothes were spotlessly clean. None of them was bent or worn out with work, for work was almost unnecessary. All they needed to do was to pick breadfruit, coconuts or bananas from trees around them. If they wanted variety, they could catch fish from the lagoons, or set snares for wild pigs. To make it still more like an earthly paradise, there seemed to be very little disease, and most people simply died of old age.

Wallis and his men spent five weeks in this enchanting place. As they left, "Our Indian friends, and particularly the Queen, once more bade us farewell, with such tenderness of affection and grief as filled both my heart and my eyes." On his way home, Wallis discovered some other islands in the same group as Tahiti. Cook later called them the Society Islands. He found another small archipelago which his officers called the Wallis Islands. When he reached home in May, 1768, he still had no idea what had happened to Carteret and the *Swallow*.

Carteret was left in extreme danger. The *Dolphin* had disappeared in the fog, and he was still stuck in the Straits. They had made no plans for what they should do if they were separated, so he knew there was almost no chance of the two ships meeting again. He was very badly equipped. The *Dolphin* was carrying all the things that the expedition had brought for trade with natives. Worse, she had the only forge and iron. He would have no means of repairing the *Swallow* if she was badly damaged. He encouraged his men by telling them "that although the *Dolphin* was the best ship, I did not doubt but that I should find more than equivalent advantages in their courage, ability, and good conduct."

It took four days after the *Dolphin* had disappeared to get the *Swallow* out of the Straits. Once out in the open sea, the weather was terrible. For three weeks the winds tore their sails, and carried away their rigging. Carteret sailed doggedly on into the Pacific. He tried to keep far south to look for the unknown continent, but the wind always drove him northward. A "young gentleman" on board, by the name of Pitcairn, spotted a dot of land. It was duly called Pitcairn Island. Soon afterwards, it became famous in connection with another Plymouth man, Captain Bligh of the *Bounty*.

All this while, Carteret could see long lines of waves rolling in from the south. Such high, steady waves usually came from a vast expanse of ocean. He suspected there could not be any continent there, and abandoned his search for it. All he wanted now was to sail far enough north to get into the trade winds. He nursed his battered and leaking ship on. Many of the crew were attacked by the seaman's traditional enemy, scurvy. The rest worked so hard at keeping the ship afloat that they were exhausted.

He struggled on. He rediscovered the Solomon Islands but did not realize that he had done so. They were much further west than anyone had imagined. He also discovered New Ireland, north of New Guinea. He stopped in the Dutch East Indies for the *Swallow* to be repaired. Even after their efforts, the Dutch shipwrights were doubtful if the *Swallow* was seaworthy. In spite of this, he went on. It was one of those nightmare voyages of unending struggle, like Hawkins' from Nombre de Dios, or Lancaster's from the East Indies. It shows how a captain and crew can bring a ship home by sheer will-power, in circumstances that seem almost impossible.

In the Atlantic he met Bougainville, the French explorer of the Pacific. He learnt that the *Dolphin* had got back to England and reported him shipwrecked. Two ships had been sent to the Straits of Magellan to rescue him. Carteret finally limped home, exactly a year after Wallis.

These expeditions aroused great interest in the Pacific. Between them, Byron, Wallis, and Carteret had discovered a very large number of islands and added to knowledge of the ocean. The major problem was still unsolved. Was there an unknown continent in the Pacific? The man who could answer this question would be one of the very greatest explorers of all time. There was not long to wait.

16

The Man for the Moment

T H E man who changed the known face of the world
was born in a poor farm labourer's cottage in
Yorkshire.

James Cook had no advantages except what were born
in himself. He received the most rudimentary education;
worked on a farm for a time; and then as a grocer's
assistant. At eighteen or so, he first went to sea, in ships
carrying coal from Newcastle to London. Like that
other farmer's son, Drake, he learnt to navigate among
the currents and sandbanks of tidal waters. His career
advanced much more slowly than Drake's. At twenty-
seven, he was still working on colliers, and had just been
offered the command of a ship. Instead of taking this
chance, he joined the Navy at the outbreak of the Seven
Years War.

This meant a step down, for he had to join as an able
seaman. It meant accepting bad food, low pay, and
vicious discipline, enforced by the cat-o'-nine-tails. His
only hope of promotion was to become a master's mate,
that is a navigator. Cook was not an impulsive man, but
a quite exceptionally balanced and sensible one. He
must have felt that the risk was worthwhile. In a short
time, he was promoted.

As master's mate, he was half-way between the officers
and the men. He ate and slept with the men below decks.
This was uncomfortable, for they had less than six foot

headroom, and he was a tall man. He was allowed only fourteen inches clearance for slinging his hammock. Sailors did not then wear uniform, so he dressed in wide-bottomed white trousers, a spotted shirt, a neckerchief, and a tarred hat. He learnt all the hardships of an ordinary seaman's life. They were many, for as Dr Johnson remarked at that time, "a ship is worse than a jail". In particular, Cook saw at first hand the dreadful effects of scurvy.

While he messed with the men, he worked with the officers. His captain soon realized that he was more than an ordinary sailor in a tarred hat. Within two years of joining the Navy, he was promoted Master, or chief navigator. The name dated from the time when the gentleman captain of a ship might not know how to sail himself. Cook did not yet rank as an officer. He went out to Canada during the war with France, and charted the St Lawrence river. He became recognized as the most skilful navigator in the Navy. He was then sent to do a survey of Newfoundland, which raised his reputation still higher in Naval circles. The Admiralty recognized that he was a man with exceptionally accurate powers of observation. In spite of his lack of schooling, he was a first-class mathematician. They also learnt, from first-hand reports, that he was a very sensible, practical man. He was not given to showing his feelings, but all who worked with him trusted him.

The Admiralty and the Royal Society, the chief scientific body in England, were looking for somebody to command an expedition to the Pacific. They had reached deadlock, then someone suggested Cook. He was promoted lieutenant, and so, at the age of forty, began the important part of his work.

This expedition was different from all that had gone before. It was scientific in its approach from the start. The official reason for going to the Pacific was to observe the planet Venus, which was due to pass between the earth and the sun. It was believed that detailed observations would help in calculating how far away the sun was. A party from Greenwich Observatory was going to help in this. Some other civilians were going as botanists, to study plants in the countries they visited. They included young Joseph Banks, later Sir Joseph and President of the Royal Society.

The secret reason for going was given in a sealed packet to Cook. He was to search "for a continent, or land of great extent . . . to the southwards of the tracks of former navigators." In accepting this task, Cook was not moved by thoughts of glory, gold, or romance. He was a man who was dedicated to finding out what was actually there.

All the preparations for going were systematic. Cook chose a bark, or small ship, called the *Endeavour*. She was a Whitby collier of the type in which he had learnt his trade. Her overall length was just over a hundred feet, and she was just under thirty feet in the beam. She was a practical, workaday vessel with nothing graceful at all about her. Her bows were very rounded, and her stern square, so she was not capable of any great speed. Cook cared far more that she should be steady and sturdy. She was not very deep in the water, and this again suited Cook. He wanted to be able to sail her close inshore, and to beach her, if necessary, for repairs. The only structure on deck was the captain's cabin. Although she was a naval vessel, Cook refused to have the deck cluttered up with a lot of guns. In all, she was the most unromantic of ships, though John Hawkins would have approved of her.

The *Endeavour* carried a crew of eighty as well as eleven civilians. Cook had the responsibility of trying to keep them healthy. He was determined that the ship and the men's clothing should be kept clean and dry. He meant them to eat a balanced diet. Sailors' food had not improved since Elizabethan times. They still lived on salt beef and pork, cheese, and hard ship's biscuit. Their food still went bad and maggoty, and their beer still went sour. On long voyages, they died like flies from scurvy. Cook, unlike most captains, had actually lived on the lower decks, and knew all about the hardships of ordinary seamen. The Navy Board had told him to carry scurvy-preventing foods, such as pickled cabbage, or sauerkraut, and Cook was determined to insist from the start that the sailors ate it.

Cook was not the first captain to tackle the problem of seamen's health. Both John and Richard Hawkins cared deeply about it. Richard Hawkins' *Observations* are full of remarks about the need to keep ships clean and dry. He knew all about the value of citrus fruit in preventing scurvy. Another expert on health at sea was the Plymouth surgeon, James Yonge. His journal gives one of the best accounts of life at sea in the seventeenth century. Later, he became surgeon at the Naval Hospital in Plymouth, and at Plymouth Dock. He, too, knew how to cure scurvy. What was it Cook did that no one had done before? He used his powers as a captain, which gave him sole and final authority in his ship, to see that the ship was kept clean and the sailors ate the right food. On shore, Cook was a humane, unpretentious man. As a captain, he exacted unswerving obedience. The sailors did not resent this. They not only respected him, but they loved him, as earlier sailors had loved that other stern disciplinarian, Drake.

On August 26th, 1768, Cook sailed out of Plymouth. He had been moored in the Hamoaze. The dockyard was now thriving and all the wide expanse of water was dotted with ships. The Navy and the dockyard officials had created an agreeable social life for themselves, with balls and assemblies held in the Long Room. Cook sailed down the Hamoaze, threading his way through the other ships. Across the water from Plymouth, some elegant ladies and gentlemen strolled in the wooded park of Mount Edgecumbe. They glanced at the blunt-nosed Whitby collier, the *Endeavour*, and went on talking. A few minutes later, Cook was caught by the swell in the Sound. There was no breakwater yet to stop the rush of the waves. He headed towards the open sea. A fisherman out at Cawsand glanced up from mending his nets. He, too, took no particular interest. So many ships sailed out of Plymouth. There was nothing to show this was different from the others.

From the very first, Cook imposed a most strenuous discipline over health. The seamen would not eat the sauerkraut, so he had it served to the officers. This did the trick. "The moment they see their superiors set a value on it, it becomes the finest stuff in the world." When they reached their first port, Madeira, the crew was served with fresh meat. Two men refused to eat it, so Cook had them flogged. This was a cruel punishment, and shows how strongly Cook felt about diet. Although he was a strict man, he was never, in any way, a man who enjoyed being brutal.

They sailed across the Atlantic to Rio de Janeiro. Then rather than go through Magellan's Straits, they rounded Cape Horn. Cook wrote down details of their passage as a guide to other sailors. He did it so well that his directions were used right into the twentieth century. Once in the Pacific, they set course for Tahiti. From Wallis' reports, it would be the perfect place for the observations of Venus.

Tahiti was still as it was when Wallis had left it; as near to an earthly paradise as anyone could imagine. The soft sand of the beaches was fringed with palms, and brilliantly coloured flowers and exotic birds glowed brightly against lush, green leaves. Because the land was so rich and abundant, nobody needed to work hard. The young and energetic could swim in the pounding surf in the daytime, and dance at night. The older Tahitans, according to Cook, seemed "to spend most of their time in eating and sleeping".

A romantic would have been completely enraptured with Tahiti. Cook, with his mixed Scottish and York-shire blood, was not a romantic man. Soon, he noticed that life in Tahiti was not as idyllic and blissful as it first seemed. The people fought one another, fiercely and savagely. They did what they felt like doing, with no idea of restraining themselves. This soon led to complica-tions with the sailors, for the Tahitans were very deter-mined thieves. They invited a party to a feast, and picked several men's pockets. They stole Cook's socks. They picked nails out of the ships, and then made off with the vital quadrant, which was needed for the observations of Venus. Cook's attitude to the Tahitans was always ex-tremely balanced. He ordered his men to treat them with "every possible humanity". Unlike some later visitors, he never blamed them for not behaving like Europeans. There was no reason why they should. On the other hand, he was not prepared to put up with too much inconvenience. He would take firm measures to get the quadrant restored; and he did so.

The observations of Venus were duly made, and Cook sailed from Tahiti with a native priest named Tupaia on board. They sailed due south, and ran into fog and gales. Even the little pigs they had brought from Tahiti for fresh meat were suffering from the cold. For another month, they sailed on through empty seas. This was the sheer vastness of the Pacific that was so hard for the human mind to grasp. Then Cook saw that the colour of the water was paler. He took this to mean it was not so immensely deep. A boy of twelve, called Nicholas Young, climbed up the rigging to take his turn as look-out. Cook peered out into the distance, but from the deck of the ship could see nothing at all. Suddenly, Nick gave a shout. He had sighted land. They sailed on towards a point, which was given the name "Young Nick's Head". Then they entered a bay. Cook looked round carefully, noting everything that he saw. "We saw in the bay several canoes, people upon the shore, and some houses in the country. The land on the sea coast is high, with white steep clifts (sic) and back inland are very high mountains, the face of the country is of a hilly surface and appears to be clothed with wood and verdure." It was the country which Tasman had found in the seventeenth century but never explored. The Dutch had already given it a name: New Zealand.

At first, New Zealand proved disappointing. It was so steep and mountainous that there were few places to land. Whenever Cook managed to find a place, the natives, the Maoris, were angry. They came rushing out in a body, brandishing weapons, and breaking into a threatening-looking war-dance. Tupaia, the Tahitan, was able to speak to them in a language they understood. They would not listen to him. Their only reply was to wave their weapons above their heads. Cook did not despair. He hoped "by good treatment and presents . . . to gain their friendship", but matters did not improve. Then a canoe attacked one of the boats. The English fired at it, and killed two or three Maoris. Cook was very distressed. He reproached himself for having tried to make contact with the Maoris, only to end up by killing them.

He did not allow any of this to distract him from his main task. He started to chart the coast of New Zealand, bay by bay, and headland by headland. No newly discovered country had ever been recorded in such detail before. He worked his way slowly on, taking careful soundings of the depth of the water offshore. From time to time, he saw a place where he could land. He took the chance to get fresh water supplies, or greenstuff, such as wild celery, to help combat scurvy. The Maoris remained unfriendly. The English sailors were horrified and yet fascinated when they realized that the Maoris were cannibals. As for the Maoris, they could not imagine what the newcomers were. They were used to huge war canoes, some over sixty feet long, but they had never seen a ship in full sail before. They were puzzled because the sailors rowed with their backs to the way they were going. Could they be goblins with eyes in the backs of their heads? There was another great mystery. An old man, who was a boy when the *Endeavour* arrived, described it many years later. "The goblins lifted their walking sticks up and pointed them at the birds, and in a short time thunder was heard and a flash of lightning was seen, and a bird fell from the trees; and we children were terrified and ran away."

Cook sailed on. From time to time, he found natives who were more friendly, but he had other problems. Gale-force winds and violent squalls of rain often made it impossible to keep the land in sight. Slowly it became clear that New Zealand must be an island, or rather, they found, two islands. It was not the mysterious continent in the Pacific. After six months of painstaking work, they had sailed right round the islands. Banks, on his trips ashore, had collected more than four hundred new types of plant. In spite of being so mountainous, the country must be very fertile. They had even come to respect the Maoris. They might be warlike, but they were not treacherous. "We never had an instance of their attempting to surprise or cut off any of our people when they were on shore."

At the end of his voyage around New Zealand, Cook had taken possession of the country for Great Britain, and had charted both islands. His charts can be criticized in small details, but it is a tribute to them that anybody should bother to do so. No newly discovered country had been surveyed with such care and precision. Indeed, his maps of New Zealand were as good as any maps which existed of the coasts of England or France.

With this achievement behind them, they set off on the next stage of their journey. They could not sail straight back to England, for they needed to take on fresh provisions and to overhaul the *Endeavour*. The obvious thing was to make straight for the Dutch East Indies. It was the most civilized place they could find in that part of the world. Cook knew that his work on New Zealand was enough to justify the voyage. He was not satisfied. He had now sailed far enough in the Pacific to realize that there was no vast southern continent. There was still a major puzzle; the mass of land which Tasman had found and named New Holland in the north and Van Diemen's land in the south. What was this land exactly? Was there an east coast facing towards New Zealand? Cook looked at his crew, and saw they were very healthy. There was nothing to stop him from going to find out.

They sailed for more than two weeks across a seemingly endless ocean. Then they saw what might be signs of land: a butterfly and a small land bird. The weather was very squally, and it was impossible to see far ahead. Then Lieutenant Zachary Hicks caught sight of land through the rain. The place was given the name Point Hicks. They sailed northwards up the coast. There was a strong wind blowing, and the surf pounded heavily on the shore. There was no hope of landing. They were near enough to see groups of men on the shore. Soon they were commenting on how strangely the men were behaving. Everywhere else they had been, the natives had been excited by the *Endeavour* with her billowing white sails. These men showed neither fear nor excitement. Their lack of curiosity was almost uncanny.

At last, they discovered a bay in which they could land. They gave it the name Stingray Harbour. After they had stayed there a while, Banks became more and more enthusiastic about the large number of new plants he found. The name of the place was changed to Botany Bay. Meanwhile, the natives became actively hostile. They had ignored the *Endeavour* as being something too strange for them to comprehend. When they saw men with white faces; to the natives the colour of death; they treated them as obvious enemies. Cook tried in vain to get on good terms with them. He produced little presents and trinkets, like beads, ribbons and nails. The Tahitans had been delighted with such things. These natives ignored them completely.

The *Endeavour* sailed on north. They passed a natural harbour which they called Port Jackson. Under the name of Sydney, it was to become one of the finest harbours anywhere in the world. They passed a promontory which they named Cape Byron, after Foul Weather Jack. All this time, they were keeping very close to the coast, so that they could survey it and land whenever they saw a suitable place. Cook noticed apprehensively that between them and the open sea there was a reef of coral, spiky and sharp as metal. He kept on looking at it, hoping that it would soon come to an end. A sailor was on duty the whole time taking soundings. He threw a line weighted with lead overboard to find out how deep the water was. Nobody yet realized that Cook had brought the *Endeavour* inside a series of coral reefs. This is now known as the Great Barrier Reef. It stretches up the east coast of Australia for more than a thousand miles.

Disaster struck at night. Everyone except for the men on watch had settled to sleep. There was a loud grating noise, and the ship rocked uncontrollably. They were impaled on the coral, and shipping water fast. Half-dressed men rushed up on deck. Cook appeared in his underclothes, for the situation was far too serious to care about dignity. He knew that their only hope would be to keep the crew calm.

His own presence of mind affected everyone else on board. Orders were given which were sensible and coherent. Everybody on board worked together to carry them out. First, they tried to lighten the ship. They flung out ballast and guns, and then even their food and water. Still she would not float. All they could do was to wait for the next high tide. In the meantime, they had to pump to stop the level of water from rising inside the ship. One of the pumps broke down. The men who were resting from duty stared anxiously down at the sea. They saw fragments of planking which had been sheared off by the coral floating about on the moon-lit water. Cook pumped away with the men. He knew all too well that the ship's boats would not be big enough to take everybody to land if the *Endeavour* broke up.

They were stuck on the coral for twenty-three hours, then at last the tide floated them off. They still had the problem of whether their pumps could keep pace with the leak. The carpenter reported that the water was gaining on them. There was nothing that they could do. Then he found out that he had mis-calculated. The news acted "like a charm", and the exhausted men pumped with sudden new vigour. Then a young midshipman, Jonathan Monkhouse, suggested they "fother" the ship. They put a sail over her bows filled with torn-up rags, rope picked to shreds, sheep's wool, and anything else they could find. The suction of the leak pulled it in, and stopped the rush of the water. Now they could pump the *Endeavour* dry, and she made for the land. Cook told them that no ship's company had ever behaved better. He was not a man given to making meaningless statements.

It took them six weeks ashore to repair the damage. The coral had sliced the ship's timbers as cleanly as if they had been cut by an axe. The time on shore gave them the chance to make the first detailed observations of New Holland, or as it was called fifty years later, Australia. Banks was enchanted by all the brilliantly coloured birds and butterflies. He was amazed by animals unlike any others known to exist in the world. He saw a creature with a long tail that hopped on its hind-legs. The natives gave it a name that sounded like "kangaroo". He saw a strange, horned creature that looked like a flying fox.

The original inhabitants, or aborigines, became a little more friendly, though they never welcomed the sailors in the way the Tahitans had. Their skin appeared to be black, but when Banks spat on his finger and rubbed one of them he saw they were really chocolate brown. They were sturdily built and went naked, with white paint on their skin. They wandered about, with no settled homes, and seemed perfectly happy with their way of life. As Cook wrote, "They seemed to set no value on anything we gave them, nor would they ever part with anything of their own."

At last, the *Endeavour* was ready to sail again. It was only to meet fresh dangers. By skilful navigation, they managed to make their way through the shoals of the Great Barrier Reef. One man took endless soundings, while Cook stationed himself at the masthead to try to read the pattern of the water ahead. He stared intently at every little change of movement or colour. "We were surrounded on every side by dangers, in so much that I was quite at a loss which way to steer."

Outside the reef, their danger was even greater. One day the wind dropped, and they realized that they were being carried helplessly towards the great mass of coral. The water was too deep for any anchor to hold. They swept nearer and nearer. The ship's boats were launched in an effort to tow them away, but the men could not row strongly enough. Then at the very last moment they saw a gap in the reef. The boats towed the *Endeavour* towards it, the men straining desperately. A wild rush of water seized them, and hurled them in through the gap. They were safe inside.

For the rest of their journey up the coast, they kept inside the reef. Then, after formally taking possession of eastern Australia, they made their way through the reef again, and headed for the East Indies. They were able to establish what had not been quite certain before; that Australia and New Guinea were completely separate places. Cook, with a typical understatement, wrote that he felt "no small satisfaction".

He congratulated himself that "the dangers and fatigues of the voyage were drawing to an end". He spoke too soon. He put into Batavia, now Jakarta, in the East Indies. There was not a single sick man on board. This was so unlike all previous long voyages that it showed the amazing success of his régime. When the *Endeavour* was taken out of the water, they saw that she was terribly riddled with worm. Cook had declined to have her copper-bottomed because this would have made her difficult to repair. She was so sheared down by the coral reefs that in places her planks were barely a quarter of an inch thick. It was a miracle that she had floated at all. The men told one another that all they needed to do was to get the *Endeavour* repaired, and then sail home.

It was then that tragedy came. During the two months they spent in Batavia, they were stricken by malaria and dysentry. Men who had survived the long voyage and their near ship-wreck died in a matter of days. After they sailed, twenty-two more men died on the homeward voyage. They were all thankful when Nick Young sighted Land's End in July 1771.

Cook was not the discoverer of Australia and New Zealand. He was the man who found out what they really were. He mapped the whole of New Zealand and all eastern Australia with an accuracy that no other explorer had ever begun to approach. He had taken with him men who were interested in scientific observation. He himself had shown an ever-awakening interest in the people and the wild life of the places he visited. Until he stopped in Batavia, he had achieved more for seamen's health in one voyage than any other commander in history.

His discoveries were not complete. He had still not finally settled the question of a great southern continent. He had shown, quite conclusively, that it must be very much smaller than anyone had supposed. He made a careful list of what he had failed to do, and concluded firmly, "This voyage will be found as complete as any before made to the South Seas." This modest and unassuming confidence in himself is typical of him. With only one voyage in command, Lieutenant Cook, as he still was, had shown himself among the great seamen of history. He had two voyages still to come.

17

Furthest South

NOT everybody was satisfied. Banks received a
great deal of praise for his scientific work. But old
ideas die very hard. A number of people still
believed that a great southern continent must exist. They
reproached Cook for not having found it. Australia and
New Zealand were a very poor substitute for the rich
and glittering lands of which they had dreamed. So
in July, 1772, a year to the day after his return, Cook
set out again from Plymouth. His orders were to
solve the problem of the southern continent once and
for all.

He was going to do this in a thorough and systematic
way. His plan was to sail right round the globe at a very
far southerly latitude, and to chart all the land that he
found. Cook had already shown his outstanding skill in
this kind of work. It would be a long task, calling for
great endurance. This, too, Cook had shown he had.
Above all, it would need some sort of driving force to keep
his ship and his men going in the hardest conditions. Did
Cook have this as well? At first sight, he seems too self-
controlled, and too much the detached observer. It was
only occasionally that he showed his innermost feelings.
In writing about the far south he declared, "I who had
ambition not only to go farther than anyone had been
before, but as far as it was possible to go." This is what
made Cook the complete explorer. Beneath all his

discipline, and his scientific detachment, was a quest-
ing spirit, like Drake's.

The *Endeavour* was no longer fit for a long voyage.
Because of what had happened when she nearly sank on
the Great Barrier Reef, the Admiralty decided to send a
second ship with the expedition. Both were Whitby
colliers of the same type as the *Endeavour*. Their names
echoed the great days of English seafaring: *Drake* and
Ralegh. Then somebody suggested that this would offend
the Spaniards, and their names were accordingly
changed to *Resolution* and *Adventure*. Cook himself sailed
in the *Resolution*. The commander of the *Adventure* was
Lieutenant Tobias Furneaux, the Plymouth-born man
who had sailed round the world with Wallis.

Both ships were got ready with great care. Joseph
Banks, who had been so much praised for his work on the
first expedition, meant to come on the second. He had
new cabins built on the deck of the *Resolution* to take all
his party, including his own musicians, as well as his
scientific equipment. By the time he had finished, the
ship was too top-heavy to sail safely down the Thames.
She would be a death-trap in the Antarctic. When this
was pointed out to him, Banks crossly withdrew all his
party, who included the famous painter, Zoffany. Two
Germans, called Forster, were appointed as scientific
observers instead. They did not prove the easiest of men
to get on with. William Hodges was to go as official
painter, to keep a detailed record of all they saw. Two
astronomers were chosen as well. Banks' additions to the
ship, which had added greatly to the expense, were
knocked down.

They had a smooth passage from Plymouth to Cape
Town in South Africa. As they sailed peacefully on, the
Forsters were able to study the life in the sea, and the sea
itself. They took out a small boat to find the direction of
the current, and lowered thermometers into the water to

take the temperature of the sea at various depths. It was the beginnings of scientific study of the sea. They also observed the many minute creatures which lived in the water. Earlier sailors, like Richard Hawkins, had written about these creatures, but the Forsters were able to study them "by the common magnifier of Mr Ramsden's improved microscope". Young Georg Forster did not let science lessen his sense of wonder. He marvelled at what he saw, such as the phosphorescence in Table Bay. "As far as we could see the whole ocean seemed to be in a blaze."

From Cape Town, they headed south. They ran into heavy gales, and the ships were battered and tossed about. Not only the decks were awash with water, it came crashing into the cabins as well. Huge birds, albatrosses, floated overhead. Their white wings were often more than ten foot from tip to tip. Sometimes they were uncannily silent, at other times they uttered a strange, screaming cry. Then the sailors saw drifting icebergs, twice as high as their own highest masts. The fresh water casks froze. The ropes froze as stiff as metal, and the sails were all covered with solid snow. It was December, the so-called Antarctic summer. Suddenly, they thought that they sighted land. It proved, wrote Forster, "an immense field of flat ice before us, broken into many small pieces on the edges, a vast number of islands of ice of all shapes and sizes rose beyond it as far as the eye could see." It was the first time anybody had seen the vast Antarctic icepack.

To make matters worse, there was fog. Two of the scientists went out in a boat to study the current, and lost sight of the ships. "They rowed about for some time, making vain efforts to be heard, but all was silent about them, and they could not see the length of their boat." Fortunately, they were saved. Then, in mid-January, they crossed the Antarctic circle, the first ships ever to do

so in all human history. For three weeks longer they cast
around, trying every likely-looking gap in the ice. They
could find no open sea to carry them even further south.
Still there was muffling, blanketing fog. The two ships
lost one another. The men shouted, but the fog deadened
all noise. Both captains decided to follow their emergency
plans, to meet again in Queen Charlotte's Sound between
the North and South Islands of New Zealand.

The early voyages to America had inspired *The
Tempest*. This journey to the Antarctic was also to pro-
duce a poetic record, in one of the strangest, most haunt-
ing poems ever written. In the *Rime of the Ancient Mariner*,
Coleridge, who was born in the year the expedition set
sail, echoes the words and sensations of Forster and Cook.

"And now there came both mist and snow
And it grew wondrous cold:
And ice, mast-high, came floating by,
As green as emerald.

And through the drifts the snowy clifts
Did send a dismal sheen:
Nor shapes of men nor beasts we ken—
The ice was all between.

The ice was here, the ice was there,
The ice was all around:
It cracked and growl'd, and roared and howl'd
Like noises in a swound!

At length did cross an Albatross
Thorough the fog it came;
As if it had been a Christian soul,
We hail'd it in God's name."

Cook set his course for New Zealand. He arrived at the
rendezvous to find Furneaux already there. At the time

when they met, none of Cook's men were sick, in spite of the dreadful conditions that they had been through. Furneaux's men had already had some time on land to recover, and to eat fresh greenstuff. In spite of this, a number of them were ill. The difference was in the character of the captains. Furneaux did not use an iron discipline to impose strict rules about diet.

Their first season of major exploration was over. Cook had now surveyed rather more than one third of Antarctic waters, that is to say the section between South Africa and New Zealand. He had shown quite conclusively that there was no continent in that part with anyone living on it. After such a terrible summer, he knew that it would be impossible to explore there during the winter. Cook therefore decided to spend the coming months cruising among the South Sea Islands. It would refresh his men, and add to knowledge of the Pacific at the same time. He went to Tahiti again, and Furneaux took on board a young native called Omai. He was the successor of the American Indians whom the Elizabethan voyagers used to take home. They sailed on to another group of islands called Tonga. The natives were so welcoming that the place has been known ever since by the second name of the Friendly Islands.

Once again, the *Resolution* and the *Adventure* were separated. This time, they never succeeded in finding each other. Furneaux had some hideous adventure with cannibals. Several of his crew were killed and eaten. He decided to sail home. He was the first man ever to sail round the world from west to east, and the first who ever sailed round it in both directions. When he got home, he introduced Omai, the Tahitan, into London society. He proved an enormous success. He was even introduced to King George III, whom he greeted with the words, "How do, King Tosh."

Furneaux died in his forties. He was buried in his

family vault at Stoke Damerel church in Plymouth. The memorials to his family can still be seen there, among many others to sailors and dockyard workers which tell of Plymouth's long links with the Navy. He is commemorated also by the fact that the name of his birthplace, Swilly, is given to a place in Tasmania. While he is, inevitably, overshadowed by Cook, he deserves to be remembered as one of the long succession of Plymouth men who played their part in opening up the sea routes of the world.

While Furneaux was sailing back home, Cook set out on the second stage of his explorations. He was now going to investigate a second section of the extreme south of the world: the area between New Zealand and Cape Horn in South America. He would be able to show finally if there was a continent hidden there. What he found were icebergs, and more fog. There was so much snow that not only the sails, but the men themselves, became coated with frozen snow. They had been issued with warm clothing, but it was not enough to keep out the cold. Instead, it became coated with ice until it was as solid and hard as armour. The men's beards and eyebrows froze. It was dangerous to be on deck, for heavy lumps of ice crashed down from the rigging.

They went deep within the Antarctic circle. Still, all they could see was ice. Once again, Cook summed up his feelings without any show of emotion. "I will not say it was impossible anywhere to get further to the south, but the attempting it would have been a dangerous and rash enterprise, and what I believe no man in my situation would have thought of. It is indeed my opinion, as well as the opinion of most on board, that this ice extended quite to the Pole, or perhaps joins to some other land to which it has been fixed from the creation." Cook's suspicions were right, and the mysteries of the Antarctic continent were only solved by overland exploration, starting more than a century later. The most famous British explorer of the Antarctic, Captain Scott, was another native of Plymouth.

Cook sailed northwards to warmer waters again. He had now been round two thirds of Antarctica. He had to consider whether to head for home. It would have been reasonable to assume that the remaining third area was no different from the others. There was a limit as to what men could be asked to endure. Cook was not a man who gave up easily. "For me at this time to have quitted this Southern Pacific Ocean, with a good ship, expressly sent out on discoveries, a healthy crew and not in want of either stores or provisions, would have been betraying not only a want of perseverence, but judgement . . . for although I had proved that there was no continent, there remained nevertheless room for many large islands in places wholly unexplored and many of those which were formerly discovered are but imperfectly explored and their situation as imperfectly known."

Obviously, the crew would need several months in a warmer climate before he could ask them to face the horrors of the Antarctic again. Although they had still kept scurvy at bay, everyone on the *Resolution* was suffering from exposure to extreme cold. As they sailed northwards, Cook himself fell ill with a "bilious colic". For a while, the whole ship's company despaired for his life. There was no doubt that this stern, almost bleak man inspired a profound devotion among those who knew him well and shared dangers with him. To their great joy, he recovered.

Once in warmer waters, they headed westwards. They called in at one of the strangest places ever seen by all the generations of English sailors who ranged the world. It was a remote and desolate island where only a few hundred unskilled natives lived. The Dutchman who had discovered it called it Easter Island. What made the place so remarkable were the huge stone figures, some as high as a house of three or four storeys. The civilization that had made them had disappeared. Hodges, the expedition's artist, painted a picture of some of these figures. It shows the strange, brooding quality, which makes them unlike anything else in the world.

Cook sailed on into the tropics. He rediscovered the Marquesas islands. They had been known before but no one had ever been certain just where they were in all the vast stretch of ocean. Cook was able to fix their exact position. This, undramatic as it seems at first sight, was one of the most important aspects of his second expedition.

Up to that time, there had been no certain method of measuring longitude, the distance from east to west. The commonest method was to heave a piece, or a "log", of wood overboard, attached to a string which was marked off with knots of ribbon. The string was played out into the water, while an officer, armed perhaps with a sand-glass, measured how fast the knots went over the side of the ship. The number of knots per hour was taken to show the ship's speed. This, in turn, was used to calculate how far she had travelled. The practice led to the terms "knots" and "writing up the log" which are still used in ships today. It was, to say the least of it, a rough and ready method. Sailors were greatly handicapped by not knowing how far they had to go. The most famous example of this is the miscalculation of the width of the Pacific. They also found it impossible to fix the exact position of new discoveries. This is why islands in the Pacific were found and then lost again.

There was another technique of measuring longitude, which Cook himself had used on his previous voyage. This was by taking observations of the moon. It was a complicated procedure and beyond the powers of some captains. Not all were born mathematicians like Cook.

The third method of measuring was now used for the first time. Cook had a chronometer, which consisted of two watches. One showed the time at the longitude O°, that is Greenwich Mean Time. The other showed the time by the sun at sea in whatever place the ship was. The difference between the two gave the distance east or west of Greenwich. A Yorkshireman, John Harrison, had spent over fifty years working on the chronometer. The final model, which Cook used, was built by the watchmaker. It took him seventeen years. The result of this work was a marvellous instrument, which stood up to all extremes of heat in the tropics and cold in the Antarctic circle. It lost less than eight minutes in over three years at sea. Two things prove how successful the chronometer was. One is that it was not until 1969 that the Royal Navy gave up the use of chronometers in favour of smaller watches. The other is that the actual model which Cook used, "our never-failing guide" as he called it, has been restored and is still ticking away at Greenwich today.

This then, was another major achievement of Cook's second voyage. Distance could now be measured accurately and simply. Exploration became an exact science and not a matter of guess-work. The scientific instrument was developed at exactly the right moment when there was a scientifically-minded commander to use it.

The *Resolution* sailed on through the tropics. They left the Marquesas where Cook had found "without exception the finest race of people in this sea." Once more they visited Tahiti and the Friendly Islands. Hodges made more paintings, which along with many other relics of Cook's voyages are now displayed at Greenwich. Then they visited the islands to which Cook gave the names of New Hebrides and New Caledonia. This was little compliment to the Scots, for the natives were, Cook declared, "the most ugly, ill-proportioned people I ever saw." They were, however, for a change, strictly honest. Then, once again, they sailed back to New Zealand, to start the last phase of their journey.

Cook had now explored two thirds of the southern ocean, all the way eastwards from Africa to South America. There remained only the stretch from South America to Africa, that is, the far southern part of the Atlantic. Cook set a direct course to Cape Horn, where the crew passed a chilly Christmas. Then yet once again, they sailed on into an ocean of ice, mist and snow. They found barren islands: South Georgia and the South Sandwich group. At last, even Cook's determination had had enough. He gave way to the irritability which was one side of his character. He said of the supposed southern continent, "to judge the bulk by the sample, it would not be worth discovery". They headed towards Cape Town from where they had begun their Antarctic explorations. The *Resolution* got back to England just over three years after she sailed.

Cook's second voyage had not discovered anything as exciting as Australia and New Zealand. If anything, it was even more remarkable than his first journey. He had finally proved that no big, inhabited continent existed in the South Seas. This had taken determination and endurance of the highest possible order. He had succeeded in measuring longitude accurately. This might not seem very important to landsmen, but it would transform life for all future navigators.

He had achieved something else. Three men were killed in accidents on the voyage, and one died of natural causes. Not a single one died of scurvy. This ugly and cruel disease had, in the past, killed thousands and thousands of seamen of all nations. It attacked ships which were only away from land for a few weeks. Cook had been away for three years. He had sailed a distance equivalent to three times round the world. He had proved that the disease could be conquered. The Royal Society elected him as a Fellow, and gave him a gold medal. In fact, Cook had not solved the scientific problem of scurvy. That was not done until the twentieth century, when Sir Frederick Gowland Hopkins showed it was due to a lack of vitamin C. What Cook had done was to solve the whole human problem. Before he sailed, men had died on every long voyage, their bodies swollen so that they could not breathe or eat, their bleeding gums rotting away. Cook, by sheer force of his character and the discipline he imposed, had shown that this need never be so again. He had performed an immense service to humanity.

18

The Last Journey

AT LAST, Cook became really famous. He was promoted to Captain, and given a shore post at Greenwich Hospital. This pleased one person at least, Mrs Cook. Her life was an obscure one, devoted to wondering how her husband was getting on, and dealing, as best she could, with the serious illnesses of her six children. Cook himself was less certain. "A few months ago the whole southern hemisphere was hardly enough for me, and now I am going to be confined within the narrow limits of Greenwich Hospital, which are far too small for an active mind like mine." He need not have worried.

In his two brilliant voyages, Cook had disposed of a myth that had lingered since Elizabethan times: the idea of a great continent in the southern seas. There remained another myth which was equally strong. This was the idea of a North-West Passage through North America, between the Atlantic and the Pacific. If it really existed, it would provide the shortest route between Europe and the Far East. The Admiralty decided to send an expedition to clear up the matter once and for all. Who should lead it but Cook?

Once again, he was to take the *Resolution* and the *Discovery*. The crews were chosen. Charles Clerke, who had served under Cook in the *Endeavour*, was to command the *Discovery*. Another man who had sailed with Cook before was the young midshipman, George

Vancouver. He was later to become famous as an explorer himself, and was to give his name to a city in Canada. The Master, that is the navigator, of the *Resolution* was William Bligh. Bligh was a Plymouth-born man, who later won a somewhat uneasy fame. He was the central figure of one of the most celebrated rebellions of all time: the mutiny of the *Bounty*.

This time, Cook did not carry a party of scientists. After the stimulus of his earlier voyages, he was developing into a skilled scientific observer himself. He had started off as a famous navigator, with a talent for mathematics. As he travelled, he became interested in plants and animals and in people. He wrote records of what people looked like, how they lived, and what their religious customs were. Cook's *Journals* are impressive for their balanced and tolerant tone. He accepted strange people for what they were, and not for what he felt they ought to be like. He met cannibals and he met thieves. While he disliked both cannibalism and thieving, he managed to see these people in relation to their own background. He did not attempt to judge them by standards that they had never heard of themselves. In any case, he once pointed out, travellers do not always meet the best people in the countries they visit. He would not want England judged by the men and women who haunt the waterfronts of our seaports. His whole attitude to the people he met is summed up in the directions he gave the sailors on his first voyage: "To endeavour by every fair means to cultivate a friendship with the natives, and to treat them with every imaginable humanity."

So, once again, Cook sailed away from Plymouth. It was July, 1776. Plymouth Sound and the Hamoaze were crowded with men of war. Red-coated sailors thronged the decks. War-horses were being taken on board. They neighed with panic at the strange, unfamiliar feeling of the moving deck beneath them. As the ships jostled together, the men called out to ask one another where they were going. The soldiers were bound for America where the colonies had rebelled against British rule. Cook's men paused in their final preparations to wave goodbye to the fleet as it sailed. There were three Navy ships to act as escort, and more than sixty to transport troops. They spread out in the Sound until all the water was dotted with their white sails. Cook watched unhappily. With a show of feeling that was unusual for him, he remembered how America had been "discovered and settled by our countrymen in the last century." It was a moment for remembering ghosts: Grenville and Ralegh, who had sailed those same waters; the Pilgrim Fathers who had started their journey in Plymouth; Gorges, of Plymouth Fort, who had dreamed of New England.

A strong north-west wind gusted, and blew the ships out to sea. The soldiers on board told each other confidently that they would soon settle the colonists. No one yet knew that two days before the rebels had issued "The Unanimous Declaration of the Thirteen United States of America." A new nation had been born.

Cook soon became absorbed in the details of his own journey. He took the now familiar route round the Cape of Good Hope to New Zealand. From there, he sailed north to the Friendly Islands and to Tahiti. He left the Tahitan, Omai, whom Furneaux had brought to Britain, behind on a neighbouring island. After all his social successes in England, Omai was in an exalted state; rather alarmingly so.

They crossed the Equator into the northern Pacific. In an unfortunate moment, they discovered a new group of islands. Cook called them the Sandwich Islands, after the First Lord of the Admiralty and pioneer sandwich eater. They are now better known as the Hawaii islands.

The islanders greeted Cook with profound awe. Like

9. A model of Cook's ship, the *Endeavour*

10. Plymouth Dock, or Devonport, from which Cook and Darwin sailed

City Museum and Art Gallery, Plymouth; photo Tom Molland

the Maoris when they first saw him, they recognized the natural dignity of his tall, rather spare figure. They sensed his great powers of leadership and his command over his men. Mutiny had been a constant danger ever since long-distance voyaging started, yet Cook's crews followed him willingly on the longest journeys ever accomplished. They were aware that, somehow, he was a man set apart. Other people had noticed this, and simply thought that Cook, who could be friendly enough on occasion, was also a little aloof. The Hawaiians took it to mean that he might be a god.

They left Hawaii and sailed up the west coast of America. They were aiming first at Drake's old harbour of Nova Albion. Once again, past and present had come together, uniting the generations of men who had sailed out of Plymouth into an ever-developing pattern. Then they sailed on northwards in bad weather. They went beyond where Drake could ever have gone. When they landed, they met Indians, who were entirely different in their customs from the east coast Indians whom the early settlers had known. Two things which Cook noticed were the feather head-dresses which they wore on special occasions, and their custom of painting and carving tree trunks. One of these, he commented, was "a truly monstrous figure". Although these totem-pole Indians were not known until Cook had visited them, it is they, not the east coast Indians, who now provide most people's idea of what the original inhabitants of North America were like.

On they went, north, and still further north. As they sailed, Cook was charting the coasts of Canada and Alaska with all his usual skill and care. Every time they came to an inlet that looked promising, they sailed down it. Perhaps here at last was the mouth of the longed-for passage. Every time, the inlet became too narrow, or a steep cliff blocked their way. Was the passage another

6

dream and no more real than Terra Australis? Still they sailed on, and still Cook wrote down details of everything that he saw. The more he travelled, the more the range of his curiosity widened.

They went through the Bering Straits, the narrow gap that divides Russia from America. Soon, they were inside the Arctic circle. The weather was very gloomy, but there was a strange brightness on the horizon. It showed they were nearing the ice fields. The men who had been with Cook in the Antarctic knew all too well what to expect. Their rigging froze. Fog hung clammily over them as they drifted through pack ice. Shapes were flattened, and it was hard to judge distances. Strange roars came out of the gloom, as herds of walruses on the ice floes bellowed to one another. Cook, ever anxious to find supplies of fresh food, insisted that some should be killed. The men found them preferable to salt meat, though even Cook had to admit that "the flesh has rather a strong taste".

At last, they reached a point where they could go no further. There was nothing ahead but ice. Although it was only the end of August, the weather was getting worse, as if the Arctic winter would soon be upon them. Cook knew that he had now been both as far north and as far south as was possible in the ships of his time. No one before had ever been so close to both ends of the world. He turned southwards again.

Cook was never to know the end of the story about the North-West Passage. In the nineteenth century it was found that a route of some sort does exist between the Atlantic and the Pacific. It is a perilous way through ice, and is of no practical use for ordinary ships. The problem of navigating around the far north of America became important once again recently. Oil has been found in Alaska and there is the question of how best to ship it.

When Cook left the Arctic he knew he would have to

wait until the next summer before he could go back again. He was concerned about the state of the *Resolution*. Wooden ships decayed very rapidly, and this second voyage in Polar waters was proving too much for her. For the first time on one of his voyages, his crew was becoming restless. Cook, not the most even-tempered of men, felt irritable with them. Their best hope was a good rest. The nearest place with a pleasant climate was the Hawaii islands. They landed there, hoping to spend a few months.

This time, the islanders greeted Cook as a god. For a little while, all went well, and then reaction set in. The islanders became tired of supplying food. They noticed the way that some of the sailors behaved. There was nothing godlike in that. Then one of the crew died. The islanders felt that this proved that Cook's companions were no different from themselves. Squabbles broke out, especially about stealing. The sailors had to keep a close watch to see that nails were not taken out of the ships. Then one of the ship's boats was stolen. Cook, as ever, was anxious to treat the natives fairly and kindly. He felt, though, that if he let them get away with stealing the boat, there might be no limit to what they would steal next. He decided to take firm measures.

Cook's usual method on such occasions was to take an important chief as a hostage. This time, the old king agreed to be one. He would go with Cook to the *Resolution* and would not be allowed off again until the boat was returned. The king set off quite happily with Cook walking beside him.

As they drew near to the water, they found crowds of natives gathered. They were talking among themselves with a low, hostile growl. Nobody dared approach Cook, who dominated the scene with his amazing personal authority. They went still nearer the water, where boats were waiting to take them off. The angry murmur grew louder, but nobody moved. The English sailors fingered their guns.

Then suddenly, two things happened. One of the king's wives flung herself on him, with entreaties not to get into the boat. Two young chieftains seized him and stopped him from moving. Cook pleaded with him in vain. Just as Cook had decided to go off without him, a messenger rushed up in a state of wild agitation. Trouble had broken out on the other side of the bay. The sailors had shot a Hawaiian chief. The news spread through the crowd. Their anger, which had been seething before, burst out. They started to hurl stones. Without waiting for Cook's orders the sailors fired. Angry howls came from the crowd. Everything was confusion. For one moment it looked as if Cook might calm the natives, then he turned his back to them to speak to the men in the boats. At that moment, they struck. All his men knew was that Cook fell with his face in the water. The natives surrounded him, shouting wildly. They dragged him on to the beach, and then set on him, like a pack of hounds on their prey.

Cook's body was never recovered, though his crew were given a few bones and his hands. One of his hands had an old scar, by which they identified it. So far as anybody could tell, his other remains were venerated by the islanders. They still thought of him as some superior being. Even those who had actually seen him killed, thought that he might return.

As for his men, "they cried out with tears in their eyes that they had lost their father."

Cook's discipline did not die with him. The men knew that he would have wanted them to carry on. So first under Clerke, who died, and then under Gore, they sailed once again into Arctic waters. They found nothing new. All this time, they continued Cook's strict regime on health. They took care with diet, they dried out the ships regularly, they carried burning coals down into the foul lower part of the ships to start a current of air. Their behaviour shows the sort of spirit that there was on the expedition. They continued with all this determination and care until they got back to England more than four years after they had left. It was the fittest tribute that they could pay to Cook's memory.

Cook was not an easy man to get on with. He had nothing of the out-going magnetism of Drake, or of the young man who was soon to become the Navy's new star, Horatio Nelson. He did not talk for the sake of talking, and could be abrupt, even tetchy, with those whom he thought were fools.

Cook's most obvious qualities are his thoroughness and his determination. He writes in such a calm and matter-of-fact way that it is all too easy to forget that he was a man of quite fantastic courage. He took his ships on and on with no idea whatsoever what he would find. "One steers wholly in the dark without any manner of guide whatever." He is the man who made no fewer than one hundred and thirty-seven observations of the moon to check if his chronometer was correct. He is also the man who pointed out that no one could ever accuse him of not taking enough risks, though they might say he took too many.

It was the people who knew him best who admired him most. Famous scientists acknowledged him as supreme in matters of navigation. His men followed him willingly in the most hideous conditions. At moments, it was an act of faith to keep going. "Was it not for the pleasure which naturally results to a man from his being the first dis-coverer . . . this kind of service would be unsupportable." The crews realized that he was caring for them through all difficulties and dangers. They submitted to his cranky ideas about diet, and were grateful to him for reorganiz-ing the traditional hours on watch to give them more sleep. The further they sailed, the more his true stature appeared.

In just over ten years, Cook solved the mysteries of the Pacific which had vexed men for centuries. His explorations had covered nearly half the face of the world. It was the most amazing achievement since Magellan had set out to sail round the world for the first time. By a tragic coincidence, Magellan also was murdered by natives in the Pacific.

As well as changing the known face of the world, Cook left a detailed account of the places he visited. His descriptions are so calm and balanced that they almost hide something very important about him. That is his humanity. When he met people of other races, he did not try to exploit them; he was not sentimental about them; nor did he try to reform them. He accepted them as they were, and he valued them as human beings.

Of the many fine seamen who have sailed out of Plymouth, Cook was the greatest of all.

19

War and Peace

WAR came with France, under Napoleon Bonaparte. All Plymouth was caught up in activity. In the Dockyard, shipwrights hammered away day and night. Rumours flew round the town, and every stranger who wanted to know what was happening was suspected as a French spy. From up on the Hoe, the water looked thick with shipping. The masts were as close together as if some forest were rising out of the sea.

In order to man all these ships, the press-gangs prowled round in search of men. They brought frightened, bewildered farmer's boys from the Devon lanes, and snatched fishermen out of their boats in Cawsand Bay. In one day, a fleet of forty trawlers lost two thirds of their crews.

There was wild excitement when Nelson appeared in Plymouth. He was the greatest hero the English Navy had had since the days of Drake. Then, in 1805, the news of Trafalgar came. An actor rushed on to the stage in Plymouth, shouting out that England had won a great battle at sea. There was a storm of cheers, then he raised his hand for silence. Nelson was dead.

The war dragged on, and the number of prisoners grew. They were crammed into buildings round Millbay and Sutton Pool. When these were full, they were put into old, rotting hulks in the Hamoaze. Soon there was no

room even there. A new prison was built for them, on
land given by the Prince of Wales from his estates.
Princetown Prison was set on the wastes of Dartmoor.
Although it was only some fifteen miles from the bustling
sea-front of Plymouth, it was one of the most desolate
places in England. It held fifteen hundred men. Some of
the Frenchmen who were taken there passed their time in
making elaborate models out of the bones of their meat
rations. Models of ships, and coaches, even a guillotine,
have acquired high value today. Then, in 1812, an unhappy war broke out with the former American colonies,
now independent. Soon the Frenchmen were joined by
American prisoners. They were kept, among swirling
Dartmoor mists, in the building that is still used as a
convict prison.

Suddenly, there came a new prisoner, the most famous
of all. Napoleon, Emperor of the French, was not only a
conqueror, but a distinguished ruler and law-giver. He
had now been defeated, finally, at Waterloo. What could
be done with him? He had been imprisoned on Elba once,
and had escaped. Where would he be safe? It had to be
somewhere where he could not attract new sympathisers.
The place chosen was St Helena, a small, mountainous
island far out in the South Atlantic. Generations of English sailors had called there before rounding the Cape of
Good Hope. Napoleon ought to be safe there, if he was
safe anywhere.

So it was that the former Emperor, on board H.M.S.
Bellerophon, was brought into Plymouth Sound. Only a
very few people knew where he was going. A Plymouth
newspaper made speculations under the headline,
Buonaparte : the Final Destination of the Scourge of Mankind.
The waterfront at Plymouth had seen many exciting
moments, but this was one of the most dramatic of all.
Everyone who had a boat rushed out to see him on board
the *Bellerophon*. Everyone else who could afford it paid

huge sums to hire a boat. What would he be like, this "Fascinating Monster" as one Plymouth paper called him? To older people, he was England's arch-enemy. To young ones, he was the ogre who had haunted their childhood. "If you are naughty, Boney will get you," they had been threatened. He was also a myth made life: the Julius Caesar or Alexander the Great of the modern world.

So the people of Plymouth flocked round the *Bellerophon*, and they saw him. They saw a middle-aged man in a green coat and white breeches, who wore a cocked hat with a cockade in the three colours of France. He was not nearly as tall as they had expected, and his face was sallow and a little bit puffy. Any other nation might have hurled abuse at him, or even tried to attack him. Being English, they cheered their defeated enemy. The sound rippled over the water, while from small boat after small boat, kerchiefs were fluttered in greeting to him.

Napoleon, still very much the Emperor, greeted them courteously. He complimented some of the young ladies on their appearance. From time to time, he glanced at a young man of twenty or so, who sat in a dinghy sketching him. After a while, he started to pose consciously, and arranged that the artist should have items of his uniform to copy. The artist was a young local man called Charles Eastlake. His painting, *Napoleon on Board H.M.S. Bellerophon*, started a career which ended as President of the Royal Academy and Director of the National Gallery.

Some people in Plymouth talked of the time when another French ruler had come as a captive to Plymouth. It was four hundred and fifty years earlier, when the French king had been captured after the battle of Poitiers. Most people were more interested in new rumours. There was a plot to bring Napoleon off the *Bellerophon*, and on to English soil. His sympathizers were trying to call him as a witness in a libel action. A lawyer, in a small boat, was rowing round and round the *Bellerophon*, trying to serve the writ. What would happen if once Napoleon landed in England? Before anything could, the English authorities acted. They were taking no risks, and they were tired of the show of sympathy to the enemy. The *Bellerophon* was ordered to draw clear of the crowds.

So Napoleon sailed from Plymouth, on the first stage of his journey to exile and death.

All this while, the appearance of Plymouth was changing. Devonport grew bigger and bigger, as it made money in the war. A gifted architect called John Foulston had just started work in Plymouth. His buildings gave Plymouth and Devonport, still counted as separate towns, a distinctive character which they kept until the air-raids of the Second World War.

More important for sailors, the Sound was changing as well. For centuries, it had been dangerous to approach, because of an almost submerged rock called the Eddystone, fifteen miles out to sea. At the end of the seventeenth century, a wooden lighthouse was built there, among the twisting, eddying currents. It collapsed seven years later, in a violent storm. Everybody on board was killed. Another wooden lighthouse was built, and was burnt down some forty years later.

Then, shortly before Cook sailed, John Smeaton built a third lighthouse made of granite. It survived for over a hundred years, until the rock underneath it crumbled. It was then dismantled and rebuilt on Plymouth Hoe. The fourth Eddystone lighthouse is still standing, while "Smeaton's tower" is a conspicuous landmark on Plymouth's shoreline.

The Eddystone lighthouse did not solve the greatest problem, which had existed since the first little ships had huddled for shelter in Sutton Harbour. When strong westerly gales blew, the sea came crashing into the Sound. It hurled ships up on to the rocks under the Hoe. It wrecked them as the sea poured up the estuaries of the Tamar or Plym where they were riding at anchor. During the wars with Napoleon, the English fleet often used Torbay as an anchorage in rough weather. The people of Plymouth started to wonder. The westerly winds had helped to make the town's fortune. Could the westerly gales destroy it?

The only hope was to stop the waves from coming into the Sound. In 1812, work on a breakwater started, directed by John Rennie. Limestone was taken from quarries nearby, and tipped into the Sound, about three miles south of the Hoe. By the time Napoleon was there, three years later, he could have seen the stone showing at low water. Then a great storm shifted it on the sea bed. The designers carried on with their plans. A still fiercer storm raged a few years later. Twenty-five ships were driven on to the rocks of the foreshore, and men were tossed into the seething water within sight of harbour. When the storm died down it was discovered that two hundred thousand tons of stone in the breakwater had been displaced.

This time, the engineers decided that they would work with, not against, the sea. They altered the angle of the outer wall so that it had a more gradual slope to the waves. Instead of the former straight line, they bent both ends of the breakwater like a bow. The work was not finally finished until 1841. By then, four million tons of limestone had been used, and three million tons of granite were used for facing the walls. All the trouble proved fully worth-while, for ever since Plymouth Sound has provided a sheltered anchorage in rough weather.

Among those who sailed out past the breakwater as it

was being built were men and women starting new lives in new countries. For two hundred years, the American colonies were the traditional place for the British to go. Then, just as Cook was leaving Plymouth for his last voyage, the Americans had declared their independence. The British needed another outlet for men wishing to go overseas. Cook himself had already shown where this could be: Australia and New Zealand.

The first way in which Australia came to replace the American colonies was as a place for sending convicts. Sir Joseph Banks, who had sailed with Cook, suggested Botany Bay for this purpose. Under the vicious penal code of the time, many thousands of men and women were transported. Some were far removed from what are now thought of as criminals. Such were the six farm labourers from Tolpuddle in Dorset, who were sent to Australia for organizing a trade union. After wide agitation the "Tolpuddle Martyrs" were pardoned, and four of them landed again at Plymouth on March 18th, 1838.

After the convicts, came other settlers. If Australia was to be farmed, if the seas around were to be fished, it was essential to get more labour. In many parts of the British Isles, especially Scotland and Ireland, there were more men than jobs. Schemes were drawn up to help people to emigrate. One of the most active supporters was Edward Gibbon Wakefield.

From Australia, Wakefield turned his thoughts to New Zealand. It was at the furthermost edge of the inhabitable part of the world. Although it was seventy years since Cook had observed that it seemed suitable for colonizing, no white men had yet settled there.

So Wakefield collected a group of men willing to go to New Zealand. They were all men of good character, able and anxious to work. Some could pay for themselves; others, who knew a useful trade, had their passages paid for them. Their wives and children went with them. In command of the group, he put Colonel William Wake-field, his brother.

The colonists sailed from Plymouth on May 12th, 1839, on board a ship called the *Tory*. The next year, the Maori chieftains ceded their sovereignty to Queen Victoria by the Treaty of Waitangi. The new colony met all the difficulties and setbacks that attend any great new enterprise. The second governor was Captain Robert Fitzroy, who had commanded the *Beagle*. He ran into many problems. Even so, the colony grew and began to prosper. Other ships followed the pioneer *Tory*.

Once again, settlers sailing from Plymouth had been present at the birth of a new nation.

20

Strange Seas of Thought

IN 1831, a young man stayed nearly three months in
Plymouth. He later described the time as "the most
miserable I ever spent".

He was an agreeable young man, but not, it appeared,
an especially gifted one. "When I left the school I was
considered by all my masters and by my Father as a very
ordinary boy, rather below the common standard in
intellect." He began to study medicine at Edinburgh,
with a view to becoming a doctor like his own father. He
then realized that his father could give him enough money
for him to live without working. This "was sufficient to
check any strenuous effort to learn medicine".

He went instead to Cambridge, thinking he might
become a parson. "I had scruples about declaring my
belief in all the dogmas of the Church of England; though
otherwise I liked the thought of being a country clergyman." He worked in a very half-hearted way, giving
further grounds for the view that he had neither much
ability nor any perseverance. He did develop one quite
unexpected interest. "No pursuit at Cambridge was
followed with nearly so much eagerness or gave me so
much pleasure as collecting beetles."

Unfortunately for the young man, beetle-collecting
was not a recognized branch of study. It was not yet
possible to work for a science degree at Cambridge. Then
he had a stroke of good luck. Captain Robert Fitzroy was

being sent on a voyage to survey Tierra del Fuego in the extreme south of America. He was willing to give up part of his cabin to a naturalist to go with the expedition. It was a wonderful opportunity for study, but no established naturalist was very likely to take it on. It meant being away for several years, and the work was unpaid. Then Professor Henslow of Cambridge suggested the young beetle enthusiast. He knew that the young man had not yet achieved anything in any field, but he recognized in him great qualities of enthusiasm, and possibly something more.

Dr Darwin, the young man's father, objected. Charles was now twenty-two, and had not yet shown signs of settling down to do anything. A long sea voyage might make him even more restless. At this stage, "Uncle Jos", Josiah Wedgwood the younger of the famous pottery family, intervened. He persuaded Dr Darwin to let Charles go to sea. So it was that Darwin found himself stuck in Plymouth, waiting anxiously for the *Beagle* to sail.

She was fitted out with the best that Devonport dock-yard could provide. All her ropes and sails were of the best quality, and her fittings were all of mahogany. Her hull was sheathed with fir planks, then felt, and then new copper. She was well supplied with scurvy-preventing foods, for the lessons of Cook's voyages had been learnt. There were no fewer than twenty-two chronometers on board.

High winds kept them at Devonport. In spite of the partly built breakwater it was too rough to put out to sea. They finally got away on December 27th, 1831. Most of the crew were still suffering from having celebrated Christmas rather too lavishly. Darwin was thankful to leave Plymouth. During the months of wait-ing, he had persuaded himself he had heart disease. Now he might have something new to occupy his thoughts, and make him forget his heart. He very soon did. Of all the men who have sailed out of Plymouth, Darwin was the most sea-sick. "Till arriving at Teneriffe . . . I was scarcely out of my hammock and really suffered more than you could well imagine from such a cause," he wrote to Henslow. Three years later he was to tell Henslow, "Then to this day at sea I am invariably sick, excepting on the finest of days."

The *Beagle* carried Darwin across to South America, and he had his first sight of a tropical forest. He was overwhelmed. The luxuriant vegetation, and the rich colours of flowers and leaves enchanted him. He set to work eagerly, collecting specimens of plants, insects, and rocks which he would send back to Henslow. All the time he was observing closely, and in great detail. He made notes of all he saw. Back on board ship, he carried on trying to put his findings into some order. He had not got much room to work, but "being cramped makes one so methodical, that in the end I have been a gainer".

They sailed on down to Tierra del Fuego, in the southernmost part of America. The main object of their voyage was to survey the rocky indented coastline. Cook had now established surveying as an exact science, and Captain Fitzroy himself had already charted the Straits of Magellan. Now he hoped to correct "a most important error in the longitude of South America".

A second aim of the voyage was to return three Fuegians whom Fitzroy had taken to England after his earlier trip. They had been given the names of Jemmy Button, York Minster, and Fuegia Basket. The sight of Fuegian natives in their own homes was a shock to Darwin. "The Fuegians are in a more miserable state of barbarism than I had ever expected to see a human being. In this inclement country, they are absolutely naked, and their temporary houses are like what children make in summer with boughs of trees." If Darwin was shocked, the

Fuegians, now used to England, were even more so. "Monkeys—dirty—fools—not men," they gasped on seeing the natives. They swore that their own tribes could not possibly be like that, until they found that their own tribes were even worse. They were duly left behind, but it was an unhappy story. Jemmy fared worst of all, for he had forgotten how to speak his own language, and Fuegia and York Minister were more interested in one another than in him.

Soon after this, the *Beagle* needed repairing. Darwin and Captain Fitzroy spent the time on an expedition inland. They went up the Santa Cruz river in Patagonia. Darwin had now been away for more than two years, and in his unhappier moments he started to wonder if he would ever get home. It was only expeditions like this that gave any point to the voyage so far as he was concerned. Apart from the joy of being on dry land again, the Santa Cruz valley did not seem to offer much. It was a bleak and desolate place, just a desert of stone on which almost nothing could grow. "The curse of sterility is on the land," said Darwin.

As they travelled he noticed that all the vast plain around them was covered with shells of mussels or clams. Although they were now well inland, the shells were of the type found on the sea shore. They were still of a blueish colour, as if the plain had, not very long before, been under the sea. Then, as he went further inland, he found that there was not only one plain, but a whole succession of plains, stretching inland like giant steps. The highest was nearly a thousand feet above sea level. Even there, Darwin found traces of shells. It suggested that the land must have emerged from the sea very gradually, over a period of many thousands of years. Darwin docketed this idea, along with a mass of other facts in his mind. He was still at the stage of being just an avidly keen observer. He did not understand the significance of what he was seeing; still less had he started to find any pattern in it.

He did know that he was seeing the Santa Cruz valley with entirely different eyes from Captain Fitzroy. Fitzroy believed in the literal truth of the Bible, and had wanted a naturalist to find new proof of this. But the Bible claimed that the world had been created in seven days. It implied that both animals and man had been made originally in the form which they still had. Darwin could not reconcile the idea of a creation once and for all with this sense he had of a slowly emerging land. It did not explain the varied forms of animal life that he found. He had discovered fossils of giant armadillos. The creatures no longer existed, but much smaller replicas of them still roamed South America. Darwin still thought of himself as fairly religious, but obviously he and Fitzroy could not agree on how the world had been made. Darwin could not fit his own findings into a picture, but he thought that creation must have been some long and complex process.

At last the *Beagle* left the arid and bleak area around the far south of America. They sailed into the Pacific, and up to warm, tropical waters. Darwin went on another inland trip, and this time climbed over twelve thousand feet in the Andes mountains. The high altitude and the astonishing scenery raised him to a state of something near exaltation. He saw with amazement how the mountains appeared to be the result of some "excessive violence" and turmoil. When he wrote to his sister, trying to explain things to her in simple language, he said, "the highest pinnacles are tossed around like the crust of a broken pie". It was easy to see the effect, for the mountains were clearly striped in strata, or layers, of different coloured rock. As Darwin studied the various rocks, he was astonished to see what they contained. In some he found fossilized trees. They appeared to have grown upright, then turned into fossils, and finally been tilted to some crazy angle when the rock was disturbed. At the astonishing height of twelve thousand feet, he found the fossils of sea shells. It was obvious that violent changes had taken place since first the rocks had been made.

At last, they left South America to sail across the Pacific. After three and a half years at sea, they had started on the homeward part of their journey. Darwin looked forward to seeing the Galapagos Islands off the South American coast. It would be his first chance of seeing an active volcano. When he arrived, he was taken aback. It was like a vision of hell. Bare black mountains rose sharply, and then plunged into craters two thousand feet deep. Lava lay everywhere, in peaks and pinnacles like frozen waves. It was so sharp that it shredded their boots. Where plants could find a foothold of thin soil it was like "the cultivated part of the infernal regions". In places there was nothing growing among the tormented curves of the rock except for the spiky cactus called prickly pear. It raised its grotesque branches out of the reach of the still more grotesque creatures that writhed underneath it.

For the animals of the Galapagos were strange to the point of nightmare. There were giant tortoises that weighed as much as three men. There were iguanas, freakish lizard-like creatures, the only ones of their type in the world that could live in the sea. They would crawl around on the bed of the sea, foraging for their food, then swim up again to sun themselves on the barren rocks. The dirty black of their skins mingled with the black lava. Sometimes there were so many of them seething about together that the rock seemed to be alive. Fitzroy stared at their weird, horny manes and their long claws and tails. "Few animals are uglier," he decided. They were only about three feet long, but they were uncannily like some of the giant reptiles whose fossilized remains had recently become known. Once again, Darwin had something to wonder about.

Yet one thing, more than anything else, impressed him in the Galapagos islands. Among all the dramatic, fantastic landscape and creatures, Darwin noticed the finches. They were very ordinary small birds which were dark brown or black in colour. It would have been easy enough to ignore them. Darwin, by observing them closely, decided that there were no fewer than thirteen different kinds. The chief distinction was in the shape of their beaks, and this was directly related to what they ate. The ones with the longest beaks sought their food from inside deep cactus blossoms. The ones with the sturdiest beaks moved stones to get at their food. Some types ate insects, others were vegetarians. The thirteen different types had all developed within the isolated area of the Galapagos. Each type had its own place within the islands. In the same way, the natives told him, the local reptiles all varied. They could look at a creature and say from which island in the group it had come.

Darwin sailed home with his mind crammed full of amazing experiences. He was twenty-seven years old, and had been away at sea for nearly five years. He had collected many thousands of plants and of geological specimens, most of which he had shipped home to Professor Henslow. What was going to happen next?

At first sight, it looked as if nothing would. Darwin had had no real scientific training. He knew how ignorant he was of geology. How could he make any pattern out of his vast mass of information? To make things worse, he became ill, and retired to live a quiet life in the country. Nobody knows now what was wrong with him. He may have suffered from the effects of the voyage, perhaps even from all his sea-sickness, or his trouble may have been nervous in origin. In any case, he seemed unlikely to win much fame as a scientist. Fitzroy, the *Beagle*'s captain, became famous as a pioneer weather forecaster as well as having been Governor of New Zealand. For a while it looked as if Darwin's chief claim to be remembered would be in the names of some plants. One, the prickly, orange-flowered *berberis Darwinii*, is much grown in gardens today.

Yet Darwin was heroic. It seems an unlikely word to apply to a man who spent five years being sea-sick and then came back to live in seclusion. Darwin's heroism was in his mind. He spent more than twenty years wrestling with facts. He worked to improve his general scientific knowledge. He was well-off, and had no need to work at all, and his ill health was always a handicap. Yet, haunted by all he had seen on the *Beagle*, Darwin worked on, relentlessly. The same qualities that had driven Cook ever further southwards across the ocean sent Darwin "voyaging through strange seas of thought, alone".

All the time he worked, three memories stayed most vividly in his mind. The first was the sense of an immense stretch of time, which he had had when he visited the Santa Cruz valley and the Andes. He had felt that the earth must have taken a very long time to be formed. Next came the idea of forms of life of different periods being related to one another; for example the fossilized giant armadillos and the small armadillos that he had seen. Finally, there were the groups of creatures that were related to one another but had different characteristics. The most striking example of this was the finches of the Galapagos islands. With these three things in mind, Darwin set out on "grinding general laws out of large collections of facts".

Within two years of his return, he had his first startling idea. Afterwards, he could fix clearly the very spot on the road at which it occurred to him. His idea was that species of animals can change over the generations and acquire differing forms. The forms which survived in various places would be the ones best suited to local conditions, for example best able to eat whatever food there was available. This idea of change and modification was contrary to the accepted idea that creation had taken place once and for all. Yet Darwin, living in Kent, could see all around him how farmers produced certain types of animal by selecting which ones to breed from. Might not nature itself impose some form of selection? The animals which no longer existed, like the fossilized giant armadillos, would be those which had not proved suited to their environment.

It took twenty more years for Darwin to develop his first intuition. He had to back it with solid facts, and he had to take note of everything that might contradict his ideas. It was not until 1859 that he published his famous work "On the Origin of Species by means of Natural Selection or the preservation of favoured races in the struggle for Life". In it, he gave a detailed justification for his idea that creatures which come from some common ancestor gradually take different forms according to local conditions. Only the types that are suited to their surroundings survive, and the others die out. The name given to this process is evolution.

Darwin was not the first person to have such ideas, but no one had set them out in such detail before. Some people hailed him as being "the greatest revolutionist in natural history of this century, if not of all centuries". Others, including Captain Fitzroy of the *Beagle*, reviled him. His work upset the idea that the world had been created once and for all at some fixed point in time. The year 4004 B.C. was sometimes suggested. It also brought into doubt the whole idea that man had been created in his present form.

Other voyages out of Plymouth had altered the whole

physical face of the world. Darwin's achievement was to alter men's mental horizons. Few journeys have been such a turning point in the history of ideas as was the voyage of the *Beagle*.

21

The Inheritors

IT WAS in Plymouth Sound that a whole epoch came
to an end. Ever since man had lived on earth, all
exploration had been either overland or by boat. Now
a new dimension was being explored: the air.

The English Channel was flown in 1909. Then came a
bigger challenge: a flight across the Atlantic. Before
anyone could achieve this, war broke out in 1914. For
the next four years, countries all over the world were
preoccupied with the war. During this time, aircraft
design was advancing quickly. Then in 1919, attempts to
fly the Atlantic began in earnest. Before the war, Lord
Northcliffe, the newspaper owner, had offered £10,000
to the first person to fly from North America to the
British Isles. The offer was revived, and the competition
began.

Among the various British and American teams taking
part were three flying boats of the U.S. Navy. They were
known as NC (for Navy Curtiss) 1, NC 3, and NC 4.
From the beginning, the Americans showed the same
power to plan in detail and the same technical skills that
later marked their explorations in space.

The three planes left Newfoundland on May 16th,
flying in formation. They headed for the Azores, where
they would have to refuel. The NC 4, piloted by Lieutenant Commander E. A. Read, arrived without trouble,
but the others had to land in the water on their way. On

May 20th, the NC 4 left again, but only got as far as
another island in the Azores. The weather was very
bad, and it was not until May 20th that they could fly
on to Lisbon in Portugal.

Meanwhile, everyone's interest was focused on the
pilot of another plane, Henry Hawker, who had been
dramatically rescued at sea. Nobody bothered much that
the NC 4 was stuck once again, in Lisbon. Then suddenly,
interest in her flared up, excited by that fairly recent
invention, the radio. She was reported to have left
Lisbon. She was going to land in Plymouth Sound.
Crowds lined the Hoe, and jostled for places on Smeaton's
Tower, the old Eddystone lighthouse. Then news came
that the NC 4 was delayed again by bad weather, and
had stopped at Ferrol in Spain.

On May 31st, the crowds were waiting again. It was a
perfect day. The sun shone brilliantly on the water, and a
light breeze was blowing. All around there were signs of
the recently ended war. Wounded soldiers, in hospital
blue, lay on the grassy slopes of the Hoe. The *Indarra* was
in the Sound, bringing British troops home from the
Middle East. Another big ship, the *Somali*, was outward-
bound for Australia and New Zealand. She was carrying
troops who had come all the way from those countries
to fight in the war. The bands of both ships were
playing.

Then news came on the radio that the NC 4 was
approaching. Three British flying boats went out to
escort her in. As she came into sight, everyone on the
ships and on shore cheered wildly. The ships all let off
their sirens in a deafening blare. Cameras clicked as the
plane, painted grey with yellow wings, circled around
Drake's Island. It landed in front of the Citadel, and
white Verey lights were sent flaring into the sky. Launches
rushed towards it in a spray of foam. And all over Plymouth, everybody who could rushed to see what was

happening on the sea-front, as once their ancestors had rushed to see Drake come home.

The crew, pale in their leather flying suits, were taken by launch to the Barbican, the oldest part of the city. All the fishing boats in Sutton Harbour were decorated with flags. They landed just by the spot from which the *Mayflower* Pilgrims had sailed. The Mayor referred to the *Mayflower* in welcoming them. Then came an amazing coincidence. Lieutenant Commander Reed said that he himself was descended from Elder Brewster, and from several other Pilgrims. History had come around full circle. Plymouth, which had sent so many men to America, now welcomed Americans back. In that same year, 1919, the people of Plymouth elected a native of the United States to represent them in Parliament. Nancy, Viscountess Astor was the first woman ever to sit in the House of Commons.

The NC 4 took forty-five hours and twenty-three minutes in actual flying time across the Atlantic. Nobody sensed yet that it was the end of an era. Flight would become more and more important as a means of travel. After that would come space flight. The Captain Cook of the future would survey the moon. Once again, something momentous had happened in those waters around Plymouth that have been called "the most important stretch of water in the history of mankind".

From that moment, the sea lost something of its importance, but it still had a vital part to play in the Second World War of 1939 to 1945. Plymouth was, as in the past, one of the chief naval bases in England, and one of the principal dockyards in which ships were built and repaired. It paid a terrible price for this.

On March 20th, 1941, King George VI and Queen Elizabeth visited Plymouth to see the damage that had already been done by bombing. At twenty to nine that same evening, after the King had left, the air-raid sirens sounded. During that night, and the six that followed, about a thousand civilians died. The city lost all its chief public buildings. St Andrew's church was a shell. Thirty-eight other churches were destroyed, twenty schools, eight cinemas and a theatre, a hundred public houses, and the homes of many thousands of people. Many of the dead were buried in common graves.

The city was so badly damaged that it was hard even for those who had known it best to get their bearings. The Plymouth that generations of sailors had known had just disappeared, leaving nothing but acre on acre of devastation. The oldest part of the city, around Sutton Harbour had largely survived. At the other end of the city, many of the huge grey stone buildings which stretched around the dockyard were also untouched. One which survived was the Royal William Victualling Yard, built by Sir John Rennie who also designed the breakwater. It is one of the most impressive nineteenth century buildings in England. But between these two ends of the city, the entire centre was piles of rubble.

So it was a makeshift city of Nissen huts that the servicemen of the Second World War came to know. As well as British servicemen, there were men from the dominions, Canada, Australia, and New Zealand; places that had owed their first links with Britain to Plymouth. Increasingly, too, there were men from America, as American troops came into the district to train for the invasion of German-occupied Europe. There was a strict ban on press reports about what they were doing, but by the spring of 1944 it was obvious that something was afoot. The Sound was full of shipping, and so was the Hamoaze. From trains crossing the bridge between Devon and Cornwall, it was possible to look down and see the tightly-packed craft, camouflaged with wavy stripes. Many had netting draped over them to blur their outline. The Allied Commander, General Eisenhower, and the British Commander, Field Marshal Montgomery, both visited Plymouth.

May 1944 went, with a long spell of perfect weather. The men waited anxiously or impatiently for their commanders to give them the order to go. In fact, Eisenhower had chosen June 5th as the first possible D-day, or day for landing in France. In the twentieth century, just as in the sixteenth, everything would depend on the right combination of tides, and the moon, and the weather.

The last days before the invasion were full of anxiety. The weather got worse, and Eisenhower was faced with the decision of whether or not to postpone the whole operation. If he did not act soon, conditions would not be right for another fortnight at least.

While he waited, the men got ready in ports all along the south coast of England. In Plymouth, the Vth and VIIth Corps of the U.S. Army went down the steep slopes of a hill to the River Tamar. The road they took, U.S. Army Route No. 23, is now known as Normandy Hill. At the foot of the hill, they embarked. The busy figures of the men were dwarfed by the soaring stone piers and the lofty sweep of Brunel's great bridge over the Tamar that stretched high above their heads.

Meanwhile, Eisenhower consulted his weather experts. Reports came in of a storm that raged in the Irish Sea. The troops waited, packed in their ships, while the rain lashed down. Even in the sheltered waters of Plymouth Sound, some took sea-sickness pills. The wait and the weather built up feelings of tension. Then Eisenhower decided to go ahead, in hopes of improved weather. D-day would be June 6th. Within two hours of his decision, the first ships slipped out of Plymouth into rough seas and low, threatening clouds.

The first stage of the liberation of Europe was under way. As the American troops sailed from Plymouth, they symbolized, yet once again, the strong and continuing links between the Old World, and the New.

After the war, came a new development. Sailing for the sheer pleasure of it became more popular than ever before. Men who were tired of machines in factories, of traffic jams, of having their life dictated to them by the clock, took to the sea for freedom. Nowadays at week-ends, Plymouth Sound is bright with the many-coloured sails of small boats.

The more ambitious sailors take the Atlantic itself for their sport. Sometimes, trans-Atlantic races are held, whether for "tall ships" like the old tea clippers, or single-handed vessels including minute catamarans. Occasionally, a venture captures the imagination of millions of people. One such was the feat of Francis Chichester, who on August 28th, 1966, slipped away past Plymouth Breakwater in an attempt to sail alone round the world.

At the time, he was sixty-four years old, and had suffered what seemed like a hopeless illness some years before. He was already famous for solo flying before the war, and had won a single-handed yacht race across the Atlantic since. This time, his aim was to sail round the world at least as fast as the tea clippers. His first stop was to be Sydney, Australia. He hoped to do nearly fourteen thousand miles in a hundred days.

The lay-out of his boat, *Gipsy Moth IV* was very care-fully planned. So were the supplies that he took. He had piles of bound volumes of charts; food packed in sealed plastic containers; drink, which included beer, and champagne to celebrate his sixty-fifth birthday. The primus stove was adapted for making bread, and he planned to grow his own mustard and cress. To eat off, he had a chair and large tray set on gimbals to counteract the tilt of the boat. The ropes and sails were of terylene, less heavy to handle when wet than traditional fibres. Even so, he wore rubber gloves to protect his hands. Most important of all, he had a radio to keep in touch with the land, and a self-steering gear so that he could set the boat on her course while he slept.

These technical refinements made possible a voyage which would have been unthinkable to Drake and John Hawkins, even to Cook. None of them could have imagined a boat so designed that one man could sail her for thousands of miles, singlehanded. Even so, the success of his journey would depend on precisely the qualities his predecessors had shown: endurance, courage, and skilled sea-craft.

He was to need all these. His radio gave bad trouble for a time, and his self-steering gear went wrong. Seventy-nine days out of Plymouth, it packed up altogether. He had to steer *Gipsy Moth* entirely by hand for nearly three thousand miles into Sydney. He arrived there after spending a hundred and seven days at sea.

In Sydney, he was welcomed tumultuously. His family and friends saw with anxiety that he had lost weight, and had injured his leg nastily in a fall. The worst part of his journey was still to come. He ignored any suggestions that he should call off his voyage, and declared himself delighted with the work that the Sydney boat-builders were doing to *Gipsy Moth*. Her self-steering gear was mended and strengthened, and her keel extended to make her more steady. He hoped this would turn her into a more reliable craft than the one he had sailed into Sydney. She had then needed, he claimed, a man to navigate her, an elephant to move the tiller, and a three foot six chimpanzee with arms eight feet long to manipulate some of the gear.

At the end of January, 1967, Chichester, now Sir Francis Chichester, set sail again. Ahead of him lay the most difficult task of his journey: to sail round Cape

Horn. Even for ships with a full crew of men, this was recognized as being one of the trickiest passages in the world. For a single-handed yachtsman, it was the hardest test of his skill that could be imagined.

Long before reaching the Cape, he ran into trouble. He took a course north of New Zealand, and hit the edge of a cyclone. The sea crashed into the cabin, burying him beneath an enormous weight of water and his own stores. Somehow, the boat righted herself, but for days after, the cabin was a horrible mess of smashed and stinking foodstuffs, and broken glass.

He approached Cape Horn, the place where all the winds in the world seem to meet and battle together. To his north, was the jagged rock of the Horn itself. To the south, was the risk of ice-bergs. He knew that the waves could be sixty to a hundred feet high. He drew near in a storm and thick mist. As he pitched through the mountainous waves in the darkness, he told himself that he must stay awake all the time until he was safely around the horn.

Next day, a tiny plane with a reporter on board, braved the violent winds. It took a photograph of him as he rounded Cape Horn, with only one small wisp of sail. By now, Chichester was important news.

He sailed onwards towards Plymouth. On the evening of Sunday, May 28th, he was nearing home. Thousands of people flocked into Plymouth to greet him. They came to the spacious, wide streets and gleaming white buildings of what was now one of the most modern cities in Europe. All day, they waited for him, lined up on the Hoe and on the cliffs round the Sound. Millions more were watching on television. Gradually, they grew anxious. Would he arrive while it was still light enough to see him?

Then at last a small armada of boats appeared far out at sea. They sailed by the Eddystone lighthouse and on to the breakwater. The sky grew dimmer, and the lights of the little boats began to shine on the water. Fire-boats played their hoses, and the glow of coloured lights turned them to ceremonial fountains. Then a convoy of boats sailed in past Drake's Island, with *Gipsy Moth* in the middle. It was just light enough to see Sir Francis clamber into a launch to sail the last few yards to the Royal Western Yacht Club steps.

Everyone who was there must have felt that something had been touched in their imagination. Some people disliked what they felt was the commercial publicity attached to the voyage, but none could deny the skill and the courage of the man who performed it. It was as if he had proved that modern men were still what men used to be. He reassured us that mechanical advances and the comforts of modern life had not made us lose all enterprise and daring.

As for Chichester, he said as he landed, "When I look back and think of those great sailors who have landed here, then I am immensely proud to be considered in their company."

As characters, there may not be very much difference between the men who sail out of Plymouth today and those who sailed in the past. Their training is worlds apart.

This is a computer age. The young man who joins the Navy as an officer cadet nowadays looks forward to taking command not just of a ship but of a highly complex piece of machinery. The captain of a nuclear powered submarine needs both traditional sea craft and the skills of a graduate in engineering. So the Navy has set up its own university, the Royal Naval Engineering College at Manadon in Plymouth.

In the same way Plymouth is in the forefront of training the Merchant Navy. During the time between the

11. Plymouth in Napoleonic times

City Museum and Art Gallery, Plymouth; photo Tom Molland

12. Francis Chichester leaving Plymouth
to sail round the world

Western Morning News

Elizabethans and Cook, navigation slowly became an exact science. Nowadays it is taught as a science to over a thousand students each year at the Nautical College in Plymouth. In spite of all modern aids they still need, like the seamen of the past, to be able to steer by the stars. So they learn the map of the stars, not by years of experience, but with the help of a planetarium in which they can study the patterns of the night sky.

There is one other group of men in Plymouth whose lives are devoted both to the sea and to science. They are the scientists at the Plymouth laboratory of the Marine Biological Association of the United Kingdom. This is a grey stone building set into the slopes of the Hoe, a few feet from the Citadel walls. The object of the laboratory is the study of life in the seas, particularly in the western English channel and an area of the Atlantic around the Channel Islands and western France. Its aims are primarily scientific: to acquire knowledge without regard for its immediate practical value. As such, the laboratory has attracted men of the highest international distinction in their own fields. The work that they have done has also proved to have practical uses, as in helping seamen with an age-old problem: the way small marine creatures grow on the bottoms of ships and foul them. Another field in which the work of the laboratory is becoming increasingly known to the public is in helping to understand the effects of pollution in the seas, especially by oil.

The sailors trained in technology and science who now go to sea from Plymouth are in the tradition of Cook. The scientists who study the sea are the heirs of Darwin. Much of the work they do would be incomprehensible to earlier seamen, but all of it is built on the long experience of the past.

7

22

The Seafarer

THERE is one great mystery: why should these men have sailed from Plymouth at all? Most people prefer to stay at home with their families. Why have a few men in each generation chosen this difficult life?

We remember the names of the famous, but there were thousands of others as well. Many of them were drowned in raging storms, or died at the hands of their enemies. Others died of starvation, like those of Hawkins' men who did not get home from San Juan. Thousands perished in slow agony from scurvy. Thousands more, with Darwin the most articulate, endured the lesser horrors of sea-sickness. Why, then, did they do it? Some joined their ships because they were starving at home, and some wretches were press-ganged to fight. But most of those who endured such dangers chose to go to sea of their own free choice.

Many people have tried to explain this strange lure of the sea. In a quiet cathedral library, some forty-odd miles from Plymouth, is one of the oldest books in England, the so-called *Exeter Book*. One of the poems in it is called *The Seafarer*. An unknown Anglo-Saxon poet expressed his feelings about the sea, and his words are as true as ever after a thousand years.

He who does well in the ways of the world
Cares not how I went through a winter in exile,
Careworn, on the cold sea,
Cut off from kinsmen, hung with icicles, hammered by
    hail.
All I heard was the surge of the sea,
The ice-cold wave, sometimes the song of the swan.
I took for my gladness the call of the gannet,
The cry of the curlew, not men making merry,
The sea-gull singing, not drinking with dear ones.

The night shadow grew dark, and snow came from the
    north,
Frost fettered the ground, and hail fell like cold corn.
Yet still my heart stirs to sail the salt streams,
To test myself in the tossing waves,
To fare far from hence, seeking the shores of strangers.

My heart heaves in my breast, my thoughts turn to the
    sea-flood,
To the whale's watery country, they move widely over
    the earth,
Fervent and fierce. The lone-flier screams,
Its cry whets the heart to take the whale-way
Over the stretch of the seas.

So long as men hear this call of the sea, so long will
they sail out of Plymouth.

Some Places to Visit

The Hoe is the most famous viewpoint in Plymouth. There is a statue of Drake, and Smeaton's Tower (old Eddystone lighthouse). Nearby are the Citadel (successor to Sir Ferdinando Gorges' Fort) and the Aquarium run by the Marine Biological Association.

For associations with the Elizabethans and Pilgrim Fathers go to the Barbican round Sutton Harbour. The Mayflower Steps have a long line of commemorative tablets. The Elizabethan House in New Street has furniture of the period. Island House and a warehouse on the inner basin both claim associations with the Pilgrims and are marked with plaques.

For earlier Plymouth, as it was when Catherine of Aragon landed, go to Blackfriars in Southside Street near Sutton Harbour (now a distillery), and to the Prysten (or Priest's House) adjoining St Andrew's Church.

St Andrew's itself was extensively restored after being bombed. Rood bosses on the chancel ceiling commemorate famous people and events in the history of Plymouth. A few yards away, in Catherine Street, is the completely rebuilt Baptist Church. The original congregation of the church entertained the Pilgrims.

All these places are within walking distance of one another, and are near the city centre.

Also near the city centre are the Art Gallery and Museum with the Library next door. The Art Gallery has a Plymouth Room with old pictures etc., and the cup given by Queen Elizabeth I to Drake. The Library includes a specialist Local History collection and a Naval History library.

To see the waterfront of Plymouth as Cook and Darwin knew it, take a boat trip from Sutton Harbour up to the Tamar Bridge. The D-Day memorial is on the Devon shore just downstream of the Royal Albert Bridge.

Buckland Abbey outside Plymouth (bus service to it) is the former home of Grenville and Drake. It contains Drake's Drum and other relics, models of ships etc. Anyone going by car can make a short detour to St Budeaux Church, Crownhill Road, Plymouth to see the Gorges memorial.

ELSEWHERE IN ENGLAND

London: The National Maritime Museum at Greenwich is the most important naval collection in England. It has a particularly interesting collection of relics of Cook's voyages.

Bath: The American Museum in Britain illustrates the life of the early American settlers.

Exeter: The Maritime Museum has recently been opened with a collection of boats, and hopes to expand.

East Budleigh, Devon : Hayes Barton Farm is the birthplace of Sir Walter Ralegh.

Some Books to Read

* Books marked like this are the ones more likely to appeal to young people.

1. ORIGINAL ACCOUNTS

ELIZABETHAN

The great collection of English voyages was by Hakluyt (Hakluyt Society and MacLehose, Glasgow, 12 volumes). A handy, inexpensive selection is *Richard Hakluyt, Voyages and Documents* ed. Janet Hampden (O.U.P., World's Classics). Also *The Elizabethan Voyages* ed. James Winny (Chatto and Windus).

Sir Richard Hawkins' *Observations* ed. J. A. Williamson (Argonaut Press) is the best Elizabethan account of life at sea.

EARLY AMERICA AND THE PILGRIM FATHERS

History of Plymouth Plantation by William Bradford (Wright and Potter Printing Co., Boston) is the best account.

Other accounts include *The Journal of the Pilgrims at Plymouth, 1620* (John Wiley, New York); *The Sagahadoc Colony* ed. Henry O. Thayer (Gorges Society, Portland, Maine); *John Pory's Lost Description of Plymouth Colony* (Houghton Mifflin Co., Boston and New York); *General History of Virginia, New England and the Summer Isles* by Captain John Smith (Glasgow University Press).

The Arden Shakespeare edition of *The Tempest*, ed. Frank Kermode (Methuen) quotes the original accounts of the storm.

LATER SEVENTEENTH AND EIGHTEENTH CENTURIES

The Journal of James Yonge ed. F. N. L. Poynter (Longmans) describes life at sea from the point of view of a Plymouth surgeon.

Cook himself describes his voyages in *The Journals of Captain James Cook* ed. J. C. Beaglehole (Cambridge. 4 vols). There is a selected one volume edition of *The Voyages of Captain Cook* ed. Christopher Lloyd (Cresset Press).

Extracts from original accounts are contained in *The Discovery of the Pacific* and *The Discovery of Australia*, both by Andrew Sharp (O.U.P.).

NINETEENTH AND TWENTIETH CENTURIES

Darwin left detailed accounts of his observations on the *Beagle*, for example *Journal of Researches* (John Murray). There are shorter accounts in his *Autobiography* (Collins) and *Darwin and Henslow, Letters 1831–1860* (John Murray) both edited by Nora Barlow.

For later events, there are newspaper accounts, notably in *The Times* (London) and *The Western Morning News* (Plymouth).

The *Jackdaw Series* (Cape) contain facsimiles of original documents and pictures. Titles include *The Armada, The Mayflower and the Pilgrim Fathers* and *The Voyages of Captain Cook*.

2. MODERN ACCOUNTS

LOCAL HISTORY

Devon by W. G. Hoskins (Collins) is an outstanding history of the county.

More detailed accounts of Plymouth are *Plymouth : A New History*, Crispin Gill (David and Charles), which goes up to Elizabethan times; *The Story of Plymouth*, R. A. J. Walling (Westaway); and *A History of Plymouth*, C. W. Bracken (Underhill, Plymouth).

THE ELIZABETHANS AND EARLY COLONISTS

Hawkins of Plymouth and *The Age of Drake* (both A. and C. Black); *Sir Francis Drake* (Collins), all by J. A. Williamson.

Sir Richard Grenville of the Revenge (Cape); *The Expansion of Elizabethan England* and *The Elizabethans and America* (both Macmillan), all by A. L. Rowse.

The Defeat of Spanish Armada by Garrett Mattingly (Cape) gives a very vivid account.

Lives of *Sir Walter Ralegh** by N. Lloyd Williams (Eyre and Spottiswood, also Penguin) which contains many original sources; and by W. Wallace (Princeton University Press).

Lives of *Sir Humphrey Gilbert* by W. G. Gosling (Constable) and Donald Barr Chidsey (Hamish Hamilton).

English Seamen and the Colonisation of America, E. Keble Chatterton (Arrowsmith).

The Adventurers of Bermuda, Henry Wilkinson (Oxford).

Gorges of Plymouth Fort, Richard Arthur Preston (University of Toronto Press).

The Three Worlds of Captain John Smith, Philip L. Barbour (Macmillan).

Richard Hakluyt and the English Voyages, George Bruner Parks (American Geographical Society).

THE PILGRIMS

The English Ancestry and Homes of the Pilgrim Fathers (Grafton Press, New York).

Saints and Strangers, George F. Willison (Heinemann).

Everyday Life in Colonial America, Louis B. Wright (G. P. Putnam's Sons/Batsford) contains very attractive illustrations.

Land Where our Fathers Died, Marion Starkey (Constable).

The Formative Years, Clarence van Steeg (Macmillan).

THE SEVENTEENTH CENTURY NAVY
Samuel Pepys, Arthur Bryant (Collins, 3 vols).

THE EIGHTEENTH CENTURY
Tobias Furneaux, Circumnavigator, Rupert Furneaux (Cassell).
The Exploration of the Pacific (A. and C. Black) and *The Discovery of New Zealand* (London), both by J. C. Beaglehole.
*Lives of *Captain Cook* by Christopher Lloyd (Faber) and Alan Villiers (Hodder and Stoughton).
* *The Fatal Impact*, Alan Moorehead (Hamish Hamilton).

NINETEENTH AND TWENTIETH CENTURIES
The Last Years of Napoleon, Ralph Korngold (Gollancz).
A Short History of Australia, Manning Clark (Heinemann).
The Story of New Zealand, A. H. Reed (Reed, Wellington).
Charles Darwin, Life and Letters, ed. Francis Darwin (John Murray).
Darwin and the Beagle, Alan Moorehead (Hamish Hamilton.
Fitzroy of the Beagle, H. E. L. Mellersh (Rupert Hart Davis).
*Air Atlantic, Alan Wykes (Hamish Hamilton).
**Sir Francis Chichester, Voyage of the Century*, Colin Simpson and Christopher Angeloglou (Sphere Books).

GENERAL
Maps and Mapmakers, R. V. Toovey (Batsford).
**Journey into Wonder*, N. J. Berrill (Gollancz), an attractive account of the voyages of exploration from the naturalist's point of view.

PUBLISHED AFTER THIS BOOK WENT TO PRESS
The Hawkins Dynasty, Michael Lewis (George Allen and Unwin).
Mayflower Remembered, Crispin Gill (David and Charles).

INDEX